BREAKTHROUGH
For Unanswered
PRAYERS

―――――――――

Dr. John Aniemeke

Breakthrough For Unanswered Prayers

Copyright ©2023 **Dr. John Aniemeke**

Paperback ISBN: 978-1-965593-21-9

All rights reserved. No part of this publication may be reproduced, distributed, or transmitted in any form or by any means, including photocopying, recording, or other electronic or mechanical methods without the prior written permission of the author except in the case of brief quotations embodied in reviews and certain other non-commercial uses permitted by copyright law.

Published by Cornerstone Publishing

A Division of Cornerstone Creativity Group LLC
Info@thecornerstonepublishers.com
www.thecornerstonepublishers.com

Author's Contact

To book the author to speak at your next event or to order bulk copies of this book, please, use the information below:

janiemeke@yahoo.com

Printed in the United States of America.

CONTENTS

FOREWORD ii
INTRODUCTION iv

1. God Answers Prayers 1
2. You Must Deal With Sin 11
3. Praying With The Right Motives 27
4. Pray According To God's Pattern 39
5. Persistence And Fervency In The Place Of Prayer 53
6. Praying The Word Of God In Faith! 67
7. The Prayer Of Agreement And Intercession 83
8. An Unusual Life Of Service To The Lord 99

CONCLUSION 113
ABOUT THIS BOOK 117

FOREWORD

> Then you will call upon Me and go and pray to Me, and I will listen to you.
>
> Jeremiah 29:12, NKJV

It was a Friday night. I was new to the city, and in a desperate attempt to become familiar with my surroundings (my sense of direction is not the best), I was touring the area yet again. As I drove through the streets, I looked across the way and saw a sign in a plaza announcing a church. I noticed the lights on the building were on. Curious, I drove over to the plaza where the church was located. I parked my car and entered the building. And there it was, I had stepped into a prayer furnace. I heard the raised voices of men and women from various nationalities and tongues crying out to God. Intrigued, I stayed long enough to hear the passionate prayers of the lead pastor, John Aniemeke, as he deftly led his congregation in a series of prayers.

This experience transformed my life. Pastor John's depth of understanding and commitment to prayer stoked a fire in me. I burned with a desire to know in a greater fashion the God of the impossible. My faith had been shaken a time or two by life's circumstances, overwhelmed by prayers that seemed unanswered. As

I made a fresh commitment to trust God again with all of my life, I came face to face with the contents of this book. A man of Biblical insights, protocols, and patterns, Pastor John's book Breakthrough for Unanswered Prayers challenged me to believe, yet again, that regardless of the situation, God answers prayers. I wrestled with the contents of this book. However, as I poured over the pages I recognized and accepted the invitation to take my spiritual journey to another level by reconsidering my approach to prayer. Have I arrived? Certainly not, but I am on a spiritual pilgrimage – one I began as a little girl.

Having sat under the tutelage of Pastor John for several years, may you find in the pages of this text what I have been privileged to witness on a weekly basis. In love, he asks us to evaluate our lives and consider what may be hindering our breakthroughs to prayer – is it an issue of sin, our motives, a lack of understanding of God's pattern for prayer, lack of faith or perhaps a lack of agreement with God? Have you considered the importance of your service to God? In this book, as I have, may you find guidance to help you navigate these questions and ultimately draw you into deeper intimacy with God and strengthen your prayer life as you receive breakthroughs for unanswered prayers.

Sue P. Nash, Ph.D.
Bethel Covenant Assembly of God

Introduction

BREAKTHROUGH FOR UNANSWERED PRAYERS

Have you ever wondered why some prayers are answered while others remain unanswered? You are not alone if you're stuck in a never-ending cycle of disappointment and despair regarding your prayer life. At some point in our Christian journey, we have all experienced the frustration of unanswered prayers. It can be disheartening and even lead us to question our faith. Sometimes, we might wonder if God is listening or if our prayers are simply ricocheting back to us.

Prayer is the backbone of our spiritual walk. It is our connection to God. In prayer, we seek His guidance, comfort, healing and help in times of need. Prayer brings us hope and has the capacity to transform our lives. However, when our prayers go unanswered, it can be a source of frustration, confusion, doubt and can even make our hearts sick. As mentioned in Proverbs 13:12,

"Hope deferred maketh the heart sick: but when the desire cometh, it is a tree of life." I can attest to the fact that there is nothing more disheartening than unanswered prayers. We, all, want timely responses to our prayers. Unfortunately, sometimes our prayers seem locked in a vault, unheard, with seemingly no response from Almighty God despite the many promises outlined in the pages of scripture. *Ask, and it shall be given you; seek, and ye shall find; knock, and it shall be opened unto you: For every one that asketh receiveth; and he that seeketh findeth; and to him that knocketh it shall be opened. Or what man is there of you, whom if his son ask bread, will he give him a stone? Or if he ask a fish, will he give him a serpent?* Matthew 7:7-10

Call unto me, and I will answer thee, and show thee great and mighty things, which thou knowest not. Jeremiah 33:3

I believe there are a number of reasons why we do not receive answers to our prayers. There are times when we do not comprehend the workings and dynamics of prayer. In this book we will examine common hindrances to prayer, such as: the issue of sin, insufficient Biblical foundation and faith, incorrect motives, and a lack of persistence. We will also examine the power of agreement in prayer and the significance of a sacrificial lifestyle committed to serving the Lord.

I have experienced the joy and fulfillment of answered prayers. When your prayers are answered, it invigorates, encourages and motivates you to pray more.

Whether you are new to prayer or a seasoned veteran, this book serves as a treasure trove of practical tools and insights to catapult you into your season of breakthroughs. If you are or have ever found yourself wrestling with silence following your petitions or contemplating forsaking prayer, my desire is that this book will illuminate your long-awaited breakthrough.

Don't despair, don't be discouraged, don't give up. When you discover and stay true to the principles revealed in this book, you will receive answers to your prayers and become a beacon of hope to everyone around you. As you continue to pray, may God turn your story around today!

Chapter One
GOD ANSWERS PRAYERS

Prayer means different things to different people. To some, it's a way to connect and commune with God. To others, prayer serves as an avenue to make their requests known and have their needs met (Philippians 4:6). Some people view prayer as a way to find peace with God, cultivate His friendship, and provoke His action on their behalf. All these perspectives are not only correct, but they are also scripturally acceptable. However, I know the crucial question isn't about what prayer entails or what it can do but whether God hears and answers us. This is a nagging concern for many, including numerous believers of Jesus Christ.

In my lifetime, I have met many people who hold a skeptical view as to whether or not God cares for our well-being or if He even acknowledges our prayer requests. Regardless of one's beliefs, it is undeniable that God indeed answers prayer. No matter what someone's identity, gender, nationality, or skin color—as long as they approach prayer with the appropriate method and parameters, they can be assured that they will receive answers. I most certainly have seen God at work in my own life.

BE CONVINCED IN YOUR HEART

We are followers of a divine being, the God who takes joy in us and is unwaveringly dedicated to responding to our requests. Yes, He delights in you! Whenever a prayer is uttered, God is present to answer. This assertion may seem simple but is steeped in truth. There must be a deep-seated belief in your heart that God wants to intervene on your behalf. The God of the universe, your creator, wants to give you countless breakthroughs and answers as you live life in step with Him. As a pastor, I have watched countless times as the hearts of my friends and congregants shift from unbelief to belief in a loving and able God. In our prayer services I encourage people to share their testimonies, struggles and victories of God's help. Ever so subtly hearts of fear and doubt change to faith as they listen to stories similar to their own. In a service, someone would share how God erased a financial debt of magnanimous proportions and a week or two later, another person would stand up and share how after listening to the story shared prior, they became convinced in their heart that God could change their situation too and their debt was erased. A coincidence? I think not. It's a heart becoming convinced of the goodness of God.

Sophie had been wrestling with fiscal troubles for months on end. Despite juggling two jobs, she needed help to meet her financial obligations. One night, she cried out to God, praying intensely for help. She had been told that God was willing and capable of answering prayers, but she had always struggled to believe it honestly. That night, however, she prayed fervently, clinging steadfastly to the hope that her prayer would not be cast into the void.

The day that followed brought an unexpected encounter. While engaged in her work, a stranger approached Sophie with a sealed envelope. He conveyed that God had sent him to deliver this envelope to her. Although initially apprehensive, Sophie accepted the envelope, persuaded by the stranger's insistence. When she broke the seal and peered inside, she discovered a check for the sum she needed to clear her mounting debts. Sophie was dumbfounded, for she had never witnessed such a miraculous event. It struck her like a bolt of lightning that her prayer had indeed been answered. From that transformative day, Sophie's faith in the power of prayer was deeply revitalized. She was sure that God was there, listening and responding whenever she reached out in prayer.

Sophie's story is not unusual. Like Sophie, I want you to know that God wants to work in your life in a similar manner.

GIVE IGNORANCE THE BOOT

The devil's greatest weapon against the believer is ignorance. Make no mistake about it, if you are ignorant, Satan will take advantage of you. That's why it is imperative that you eliminate ignorance, give it the boot, kick it out of your life and become aware of the strategies of the devil. As the scripture states: "Lest Satan should get an advantage of us: for we are not ignorant of his devices" (2 Corinthians 2:11).

Ignorance is akin to a thick veil of darkness, while knowledge is a beacon of light. The adversary is the ruler of this darkness, commanding its vast kingdom. Wherever the shadow of ignorance falls, his power extends. Put differently, in any sphere where you are bereft of adequate understanding (light); the devil can seize control, regardless of whether or not you are a Christian. God may preside over your health, while the devil wields influence over your finances, marital affairs, or other aspects of your life. Winning against the devil hinges on the degree of enlightenment you access. A destructive force, ignorance has destroyed many of God's people. Hosea, an Old Testament prophet in an intriguing account, writes: *"My people are destroyed for lack of knowledge: because thou hast rejected knowledge, I will also reject thee, that thou shalt be no priest to me: seeing thou hast forgotten the law of thy God, I will also forget thy children."* Hosea 4:6

In his address to the people of Israel, God says that his people suffer destruction because of their ignorance. Sadly, ignorance can alienate you from what is rightfully yours in Christ.

> *"Having the understanding darkened, being alienated from the life of God through the ignorance that is in them, because of the blindness of their heart:"* Ephesians 4:18

When you are ignorant, you put your life in danger. If you want to know how terrible ignorance is, get into your car at night and attempt to drive without putting on your headlamps. Of course, that is a hazardous thing to do, and I strongly advise against it. However, if you do, you will likely fall into a ditch. It is no prophecy of doom; it's just how things work. You can predict the outcome with a certain degree of accuracy.

Like driving in the dark, ignorance is the blindness of the heart and mind - "if the blind lead the blind, both shall fall into a ditch" (Matthew 15:14).

BEWARE OF DECEPTION

Ignorance leaves you liable to the enemy's deception. The devil seeks not only to keep you ignorant but also to deceive you. Deception acts like a snare, luring you into a pitfall. For example, simple ignorance of the scriptures may eventually progress into doctrinal error. Once deceived, the consequences can be threatening. We can, however, guard against deception in our lives. Note the following:

1. God's Promises are Yes and Amen!

The Bible says, "...all the promises of God in him are yea, and in him Amen, unto the glory of God by us" (2 Corinthians 1:20). What does "...yea and Amen!" mean? It means that when you say "Yes!" to God's promises by faith, God says "Amen!" In other words, once you agree and believe in His promises, you commit Him to perform them in your life.

"For verily I say unto you, That whosoever shall say unto this mountain, Be thou removed, and be thou cast into the sea; and shall not doubt in his heart, but shall believe that those things which he saith shall come to pass; he shall have whatsoever he saith. Therefore, I say unto you, What things soever ye desire,

when ye pray, believe that ye receive them, and ye shall have them." Mark 11:23-24 One preacher declared: when your faith says "yes," God cannot say "no!" So, once you stand on God's promises on a matter, you can consider it done because God cannot fail to keep His word. If He promised it, He will do it. When you pray, God is committed to His word.

> *"God is not a man, that he should lie; neither the son of man, that he should repent: hath he said, and shall he not do it? or hath he spoken, and shall he not make it good?" Numbers 23:19*

2. God is a Prayer Answering God

Consistently, God's word affirms that He is a prayer-answering God. All throughout scripture God assures us He will answer. Nowhere in the Bible does it suggest even the faintest possibility that God is unable to answer our prayers.

We are guaranteed answers to all our prayers if we meet the conditions. Prayer is like cashing a check: the respective financial institutions will honor it once the correct signature is on it. The good news is that you can sign the check with the signature "Jesus."

"If ye shall ask anything in my name, I will do it." John 14:14. God promises to answer so "…that the Father

may be glorified in the Son" (John 14:13). Consider the following scriptures as further proof and assurance that God answers prayer:

> *"And this is the confidence that we have in him, that, if we ask any thing according to his will, he heareth us: And if we know that he hear us, whatsoever we ask, we know that we have the petitions that we desired of him."* 1 John 5:14-15

> *"Call unto me, and I will answer thee, and shew thee great and mighty things, which thou knowest not."* Jeremiah 33:3

> *"Praise waiteth for thee, O God, in Sion: and unto thee shall the vow be performed. O thou that hearest prayer, unto thee shall all flesh come."* Psalm 65:1-2

> *"The people asked, and he brought quails and satisfied them with the bread of heaven."* Psalm 105:40

> *"And it shall come to pass, that before they call, I will answer; and while they are yet speaking, I will hear."* Isaiah 65:24

> *"Then shalt thou call, and the Lord shall answer; thou shalt cry, and he shall say, Here I am..."* Isaiah 58:9

3. The God of Bethel

All who called upon God in the Bible obtained their answers, including Hannah, Jabez, Jacob, and many others. Jacob encountered the God of Bethel, later referring to Him as the God who answers prayer.

> *"...let us arise and go to Bethel; and I will make there an altar unto God, who answered me in the day of my distress..." Genesis 35:3*

In this scripture, Jacob urged his people to accompany him to the God of Bethel, who had answered his prayers. Jacob found himself in a hopeless situation requiring God's intervention. When Jacob expressed his desperation to God at Bethel, God responded and intervened on his behalf.

The encouraging news is that just as He answered the prayers of Jacob and many others, He will answer yours too. I realize that many people grapple with why their prayers remain unanswered. In the remainder of this book, I hope to uncover insights that will profoundly influence your prayer life.

Reflection

1. Select 2 – 3 scriptures that stood out to you as you read through the chapter. Take the time to look at these scriptures in different translations. Afterward (a) write out these scriptures and (b) write what these scriptures mean to you currently.

2. If you believe God answers prayer, pause and thank God that this belief exists in your heart. If you are uncertain about whether or not God answers prayer, ask the Holy Spirit to reveal the condition of your heart. I believe the Holy Spirit wants to help. Now ask the Holy Spirit to guide you into all truth as you read through the pages of this book.

Chapter Two

YOU MUST DEAL WITH SIN

The potency of a righteous person's prayer is incomparable, reverberating with the strength of the God who answers it. When the righteous communicate their faith through prayer, they unlock divine power. As the Bible puts it, "The effectual fervent prayer of a righteous man availeth much" (James 5:16). For those who place their faith in the Almighty, prayer transforms into a wellspring of support, solace, insight, fortitude, and spiritual fortification. Prayer equips us and caters to our needs and the needs of others. Through the medium of prayer, we discover the strength and guidance necessary to navigate life's stormy seas and shield us from the disruptive influences of Satan. Prayer is an influential instrument capable of activating profound shifts in our lives and the lives of those around us. Historically, mighty people have faced and surmounted tremendous challenges armed with the enduring weapon of prayer.

When discussing the power of prayer as revealed in the Bible, one story immediately comes to mind: the story of Hannah. A Jewish woman, Hannah remained childless after being married for several years. As the unfortunate barren second wife, she was ridiculed and humiliated by the first wife, who effortlessly bore children. In her deep sorrow, Hannah went to the temple one day and prayed to God for a son, and even promised to dedicate him to the Lord:

> *"And she was in bitterness of soul and prayed unto the Lord, and wept sore. And she vowed a vow and said, O Lord of hosts if thou wilt indeed look on the affliction of thine handmaid, and remember me, and not forget thine handmaid, but wilt give unto thine handmaid a man child, then I will give him unto the Lord all the days of his life, and there shall no razor come upon his head." 1 Samuel 1: 10-11*

God responded to Hannah's prayer, and allowed her to conceive. She bore her first child, Samuel, who became a renowned prophet in Israel.

> *"Wherefore it came to pass, when the time was come about after Hannah had conceived, that she bare a son, and called his name Samuel, saying, Because I have asked him of the Lord." 1 Samuel 1: 20*

While there is tremendous power in prayer, sin can be an obstacle to receiving answers.

SIN UNDERMINES YOUR PRAYERS

The power of prayer may be rendered ineffective if we harbor sin in our lives. Sin is among the most significant obstacles to our prayers. It undermines our prayer and places us at a considerable disadvantage. Sin forms a barrier between God and us, impeding the efficacy of our prayers. The Bible explicitly states that God will not respond to our prayers if we harbor sin. Consider these proofs:

> *"If I regard iniquity in my heart, the Lord will not hear me:" Psalm 66:18.*

> *"Behold, the Lord's hand is not shortened, that it cannot save; neither his ear heavy, that it cannot hear: But your iniquities have separated between you and your God, and your sins have hid his face from you, that he will not hear. For your hands are defiled with blood, and your fingers with iniquity; your lips have spoken lies, your tongue hath muttered perverseness...*

For our transgressions are multiplied before thee, and our sins testify against us: for our transgressions are with us...And the Redeemer shall come to Zion, and unto them that turn from transgression in Jacob, saith the Lord." Isaiah 59:1-4, 12, 20

"For the eyes of the Lord are over the righteous, and his ears are open unto their prayers: but the face of the Lord is against them that do evil." 1 Peter 3:12

"Now we know that God heareth not sinners: but if any man be a worshipper of God, and doeth his will, him he heareth." John 9:31

"The LORD is far from the wicked: but he heareth the prayer of the righteous." Proverbs 15:29

"He that turneth away his ear from hearing the law, even his prayer shall be abomination." Proverbs 28:9

If your relationship with God is strained, or your deeds fail to align with His divine intent, then your prayers may be blocked, which prevents them from releasing the dynamic power of God. This is the perilous consequence of sin.

THE NATURE AND ACT OF SIN

Sin is first nature and then an act. The issue of Adam's original sin in the Garden of Eden is central. Adam's sin separated humanity from a vital relationship with God, the divine, and plunged him into spiritual darkness. Sin broke the fellowship that Adam once enjoyed with God. As soon as Adam disobeyed God's instruction, he lost the divine nature created in him.

Consequently, humanity immediately adopted the sin nature of Satan. Thankfully, Christ's sacrifice on the cross of Calvary addressed the nature of sin. Sin encompasses wrongdoing, offense, and transgression against God's commandments and instructions. Sin is an offense against both God and religious or moral laws.

Although believers in Jesus Christ no longer possess the nature of sin, they grapple daily with sinful acts. Believers commit evil acts when they succumb to temptations. This chapter focuses on these immoral acts. Unbelievers possess the nature of sin. Thus, when discussing how sin hinders prayers, we are not referring to unbelievers who have the nature of sin. The only prayer from a sinner that matters to God is seeking salvation. Instead, we focus on believers whose sinful acts may obstruct their prayers.

Recognizing the adverse effects of sin on our prayers underscores the urgency of addressing it. Below are some ways in which sin undermines our prayers.

1. Sin Obstructs Your Inheritance

Sin prevents you from accessing earthly and spiritual blessings and your eternal inheritance in Christ (Ephesians 1:11). Prayer involves executing the promises God made to His children. Through prayer, you claim your inheritance in God. However, living in sin obstructs your access to such inheritance. It's essential to acknowledge that the spiritual inheritance resulting from Christ's completed work is only accessible to those who are sanctified:

> *"And now, brethren, I commend you to God, and to the word of his grace, which can build you up, and to give you an inheritance among all them which are sanctified." Acts 20:32*

Being born again grants you access to God's family, but it's only a means to obtain an inheritance from God. To fully access it, you must be sanctified, living a life free from sin. Choosing a sinful lifestyle prevents you from thoroughly enjoying what belongs to you in Christ. Our inheritance lies in the light, while sin resides in darkness. Consequently, sin hinders us from enjoying our inheritance and deprives us of more opportunities and blessings than we can fathom.

2. Sin Blocks Your Access to God

Sin will block you from gaining access to God in prayer. Prayer is not only about making petitions and receiving; it is also about ascending in the spirit. When you truly pray, you ascend from one level to another in God (Psalm 24:3-4). Since God is holy, those who approach Him must also be holy. But like the force of gravity, sin will hinder you from enjoying full fellowship with God. It will prevent you from reaching your proper place in Him.

> *"Who shall ascend into the hill of the Lord? or who shall stand in his holy place? He that hath clean hands, and a pure heart; who hath not lifted up his soul unto vanity, nor sworn deceitfully" Psalm 24:3-4*

The Psalmist states that only those with clean hands and pure hearts can ascend in prayer. If your heart isn't pure and you're not living a holy life, it might hinder you from reaching God in prayer. It's not your righteousness that grants you access to God. Rather, it is the righteousness of Christ. However, you cannot consistently indulge in sin and expect to ascend in prayer.

3. Sin Separates You from God

Righteousness keeps you close to God, but sin keeps you away from Him. Sin acts as a separator, estranging you from your Father's presence.

> *"But your iniquities have separated between you and your God, and your sins have hid his face from you, that he will not hear." Isaiah 59:2*

When Adam sinned in the Garden of Eden, his spirit was separated from God's Spirit and presence. Once enjoying a close fellowship with God, he began to hide from His presence. His spirit, now dead to God's Spirit, became alive to Satan—a tragic outcome. Consequently, Adam became prayerless. To hide in God is to pray, but hiding from God signifies prayerlessness. Sin will extinguish your joy, zeal, and desire for God and your interest in matters about Him.

4. Sin Paralyzes Your Faith

Sin can paralyze your faith. That is probably the most debilitating impact of sin on your prayer life. Sin creates the feeling of guilt, shame, and unworthiness. These emotions can challenge approaching God with sincerity, openness, and faith. Our faith is contaminated once we feel that we do not deserve the blessings we seek through prayer or are unworthy of forgiveness. And once your faith is not in place, your prayer becomes needless. It takes faith to please God (Hebrews 11:6) and to receive answers from God. Your prayer, therefore, is an expression of your faith. If you get sin out of your life, you will regain confidence before God and position yourself for answered prayers. Do not allow sin to rob you of your faith.

HOW TO DEAL WITH THE ISSUE OF SIN

Genuine Repentance

To fully experience the power of prayer, we must first address any sin issues in our lives. The initial step in confronting sin is sincere repentance. Christ's ultimate sacrifice made forgiveness possible, but we must genuinely repent. If you genuinely repent, you pave the way for breakthroughs in prayer and other areas of your life. However, attempting to conceal your sin will hinder your progress. You will not succeed in life or anything else you undertake.

> *"He that covereth his sins shall not prosper: but whoso confesseth and forsaketh them shall have mercy." Proverbs 28:13*

When we approach God with sincere repentance, we receive forgiveness and gain the power to rise above sin. The concept of repentance is often misunderstood within the Christian community. Some people mistakenly equate repentance with feelings of remorse. However, repentance is not merely about feeling remorse. The Bible often uses the Greek word "*metanoeo*" for "repent." *Metanoeo* signifies a change of mind for the better, involving heartfelt amends with abhorrence for past sins.

When someone truly repents, they change not only their mind but also their actions. While repentance may involve feeling remorse, remorse itself is not necessarily repentance but rather an offshoot of it. At times, remorse accompanies a change of mind, particularly regarding wrongdoing. However, showing remorse without genuinely changing one's mind is possible. A person may show remorse temporarily, only to return to their old ways. True repentance involves a complete change of mind that results in a shift in your actions. Repentance without a corresponding behavior change is both superficial and short-lived.

DAVID'S GENUINE REPENTANCE

The story of David reveals genuine repentance. He succumbed to temptation, and was sexually intimate with another man's wife. This began with David observing a beautiful woman bathing from his balcony and later killing her husband through deceit. Informed of God's impending judgment, David repented. Though he experienced deep remorse, genuine repentance began with a change of mind, not merely emotional regret.

How do we know this? First, there are no other accounts in which David is involved in another adultery or sexual impropriety throughout his life. When David became much older and needed someone to keep him warm, a virgin named Abishag was sought for him (1 Kings 1:1-4, 15b). This beautiful woman lived with David until his death. Yet at David's death, she was still a virgin. David never "touched" her in all that time? How could that be? That is proof that his repentance was genuine. David wanted nothing to do with sin again. His prayer of repentance attests to that fact:

> *"Have mercy upon me, O God, according to thy lovingkindness: according unto the multitude of thy tender mercies blot out my transgressions. Wash me thoroughly from my iniquity, and cleanse me from my sin. For I acknowledge my transgressions: and my sin is ever before me. Against thee, thee only, have I sinned, and done this evil in thy sight: that thou mightiest be justified when thou speakest, and be clear when thou judgest. Behold, I was shaped in iniquity, and in sin did my mother conceive me. Behold, thou desirest truth in the inward parts: and in the hidden part, thou shalt make me to know wisdom. Purge*

me with hyssop, and I shall be clean: wash me, and I shall be whiter than snow. Make me hear joy and gladness; that the bones which thou hast broken may rejoice. Hide thy face from my sins, and blot out all mine iniquities. Create in me a clean heart, O God, and renew a right spirit within me. Cast me not away from thy presence, and take not thy holy spirit from me. Restore unto me the joy of thy salvation, and uphold me with thy free spirit. Then will I teach transgressors thy ways; and sinners shall be converted unto thee. Deliver me from blood guiltiness, O God, thou God of my salvation: and my tongue shall sing aloud of thy righteousness." Psalm 51:1-14

Looking closely at David's prayer above, you will see how passionately he prayed for God to forgive his sins. He knew he had wronged both God and man. Therefore, he was willing and committed to making amends. That is genuine repentance. He was remorseful and had a change of mind reflected in his action. I am not talking about the type of repentance that some people do today, where they immediately return to their sin, like the proverbial dog returning to its vomit (2 Peter 2:22).

The Bible also emphasizes the importance of confessing our sins. When we recognize our sins, we should confess and repent. Confession is like verbally owning up. By being honest with God and ourselves, confessing our sins, and seeking His forgiveness, we can receive the forgiveness promised in the Bible.

> *"If we confess our sins, he is faithful and just to forgive us our sins and to cleanse us from all unrighteousness." 1 John 1:5*

Not only will God forgive our sins, but He will also cleanse us of all unrighteousness. Sin can be likened to a debt; when debts are forgiven, the records are erased.

BREAK FREE FROM THE POWER OF SIN

Genuinely repenting of our sins opens us up to the full power of prayer, making our prayers more effective, allowing us to better connect with God, and enabling us to experience the peace and comfort of a close relationship with Him. We must take steps to turn away from sin and work towards a life pleasing to God. While the blood of Jesus cleanses us of our sins, the power of the Holy Spirit breaks the yoke of sin over our lives and empowers us to live above sin. We should not only seek forgiveness but pursue supernatural empowerment to overcome sin. This process begins with a strong foundation in the word of God.

HOW DAVID STAYED ABOVE SIN

Another influential factor that enabled David to overcome sin was his dedication to God's word. He did not only repent but also submitted to God's teachings. Embracing God's word empowered him to rise above sin. This is how he expressed it:

> *"Wherewithal shall a young man cleanse his way? by taking heed thereto according to thy word. With my whole heart have I sought thee: O let me not wander from thy commandments. Thy word have I hid in mine heart, that I might not sin against thee." Psalm 119:9-11*

You can rise above sin by internalizing God's word and allowing it to transform your thoughts. As scripture suggests, God's word purifies our paths, leading us to freedom. While immersing yourself in God's teachings, consider these steps: i) seek to understand Jesus' sacrifice on the cross of Calvary, ii) through faith, regard yourself as dead to sin and alive to God, affirming this belief, iii) exercise your divine authority to overcome sin's power, and iv) commit to follow God's word. Additionally, you must embrace a Spirit-filled life.

Through the Spirit, we can mortify the deeds of the flesh (Romans 8:13). And like Paul said, "Walk in the

Spirit, and ye shall not fulfill the lust of the flesh" (Galatians 5:16). If you learn to apply the principle of repentance, fill yourself with God's word, be diligent in applying the word, and embrace a Spirit-filled lifestyle, you will be well on your way to total dominion over sin. Do not let sin hinder your prayer; get it out. You will not fail.

Reflection

1. You must deal with any sin in your life. Take a few moments to consider the ways in which you have sinned against God. Ask the Holy Spirit to search your heart. As the Holy Spirit reveals to you areas of sin, begin to repent and make a conscientious decision to move from a life of sin into a life of freedom. Receive God's forgiveness.

2. David used the Scripture to live above sin. What Scriptures can you internalize to help you? Find one or two verses to meditate on that will help you with your sin issue.

SCAN ME

Chapter Three
PRAYING WITH THE RIGHT MOTIVES

The effectiveness of our prayers is not solely determined by the words we use or the frequency with which we pray. Instead, what matters most are the motives behind our prayers. The importance of praying with pure motives cannot be overstated. Our motives are the driving force behind our prayers, shaping how we approach God. If our motive is right, our prayers will be answered, but if our motives are impure, our prayers will be ineffective. The book of James strongly affirms the place of motive in answered prayers: "Ye ask, and receive not, because ye ask amiss, that ye may consume it upon your lusts." James 4:3

Our prayers will not be answered if our motives are self-centered and focused on our desires. In other words, if your prayers remain unanswered even after addressing the issue of sin in your life, as discussed in chapter two, another factor may be at play. It could be that your motive is misaligned.

The motive behind our prayers plays a crucial role in determining their outcomes. The word "motive" refers to the underlying reasons or intentions that drive our thoughts, feelings, and actions. Our beliefs, values, and experiences shape our motives. Your motive answers the question, "Why?" It is your reason for doing something. "Motive" is also related to the word "motivate." To motivate means to provide someone with a motive or a reason for action.

Our motives are either right or wrong, pure or impure. Right motives include a desire to help others or to honor God, while wrong motives encompass desires for power, recognition, or riches. Another example of an improper motive in prayer occurs when someone desires and prays for another's downfall. For example, one might wish for an evil person's demise, but regardless of a person's actions, God wants people to be saved, healed and delivered. Unlike human beings, God's love is vast. If your motive is correct, you will enjoy answered prayers. Otherwise, you will only recycle the pain and frustration of unanswered prayers. God will never answer a prayer with a selfish motive. This is a fundamental fact to take note of.

MOTIVE BEFORE ACTION

Remarkably, not only in prayer does God seek a pure motive, but in all of our dealings with Him. He values our motives more than our actions. Of course, we all desire to do good. It is even a part of our natural inclination. Almost everyone wants to be pleasing in the sight of others and God. However, the visible actions we perform before people and God are not the only thing that counts but our motives. Individuals often expect God to judge them by their standards rather than His. This confusion is typically rooted in God's focus on the heart rather than external appearance. He evaluates every step we take based on "why" we do what we do rather than the action itself.

Consequently, what many people consider as right may be marred by their misguided motives. Even our most influential acts of kindness can be undermined by our motives. In Matthew's gospel, where Jesus preached one of His most famous sermons, the Sermon on the Mount (Matthew 5 – 7), He taught us what to do when we pray, fast, and give alms. He emphasized the importance of our motive over the act itself.

> *"Take heed that ye do not your alms before men, to be seen of them: otherwise ye have no reward of your Father which is in heaven." Matthew 6:1*

Jesus wasn't addressing unbelievers in His statement here. Instead, He was speaking to the children of God. He wanted us to understand the importance of our motives whenever we perform good deeds publicly; if we do so with the wrong reason—giving alms to gain admiration, praise, or attention, or to show superiority over others—instead of focusing on Christ, we forfeit our heavenly reward. If you allow others to praise you publicly for your deeds, their praise becomes your reward.

LOVE IS THE FOUNDATION

In Paul's first letter to the Corinthians, he emphasizes the motive of love in all that we do. Regardless of the actions you take and the extent of the sacrifice you put in to secure the welfare of others; if such actions are not motivated by love, they are as good as nothing. "Though I speak with the tongues of men and of angels and have not charity, I am become as sounding brass or a tinkling cymbal. And though I have the gift of prophecy, and understand all mysteries, and all knowledge; and though I have all faith, so that I could remove mountains, and have not charity, I am nothing. And though I bestow all my goods to feed the poor, and though I give my body to be burned, and have not charity, it profiteth me nothing." 1 Corinthians 13:1-3

In all honesty, the scripture above seems paradoxical. Imagine being someone who prays, gives, and sacrifices for others' well-being, only to have your actions deemed unworthy. Consider it for a moment. How could one be wrong for sacrificing their lives for others' welfare? What could be wrong with burning one's body for the sake of others? The point is that nearly every action can be done for the wrong reason, including giving our body to be burned. You can feed people experiencing poverty and sacrifice yourself as much as you want; if your underlying motive is not love, it will profit you nothing. It is crucial to follow God and not judge ourselves by our self-imposed, superficial earthly standards. Let's learn to judge ourselves by God's standards, as revealed in His holy written word. God's word is clear; the motives behind our actions hold greater importance than the actions themselves.

LOVE MOTIVATED PRAYERS

Just as with other areas of life, so it is with our prayers. Our prayers must be motivated by love. First, love for God, and then love for our fellow humans. The attitude behind your prayer matters more to God than your words. Without love, your prayers hold no significance to God. Typically, we look forward to talking with the one we love. You will want to spend time with them. Would you want to spend time talking to someone you don't love? If you believe God loves you, you will talk to Him, trust Him and believe what He says. This belief will significantly influence your prayers.

Are your prayers motivated by a genuine love for God or merely by your needs and problems? Don't get me wrong; there is absolutely nothing wrong with asking God to meet your needs (at least, He promised to do so); it's just that there are higher motives in prayer than simply meeting your needs. Many believers see prayer only as a means to write their ticket with God. But prayer is much more, you can write your ticket - that's fine, but add to that; look out for others. Spend time loving God. Let your prayer time be more of a time of fellowship and intimacy with God.

Moreover, as you pray to Him, seek to hear His voice on what He wants you to do. That is what it means to collaborate with God in prayer. Those who pray well will collaborate with God, becoming His agent to share His love with others. If your motivation is not love, your prayers will be purely transactional. Unfortunately, transactional Christians can't go far with God, as they lose sight of the life that He offers. Many Christians have deprived themselves of greater opportunities by subscribing to the "bless me" club. This shouldn't be the case for you. Instead, allow love to be the driving force behind all your prayers. Ultimately, those who pray with love for God and others at the forefront will reap significant benefits from their prayers.

Here are a few ways to ensure you have the right motives when you pray:

1. Re-Engineer Your Values and Thoughts

Our motive is a product of our values and thoughts. In other words, if we could re-engineer our values and beliefs by renewing our minds with God's word, our motives could also be altered. "And be not conformed to this world: but be ye transformed by the renewing of your mind." (Romans 12:2). When you deliberately give attention to the word of God and allow it to change your thinking, your motive will transform. This may not happen overnight but over time as you persist in this practice, you will get the desired result.

2. Align with God's Will

Our ultimate choice in life is usually between pleasing ourselves and pleasing God. You are either praying, 'God, do it my way...' Or you are praying, 'God, I am available to do your will." Rather than try to use God to accomplish your will, why not surrender to His will?

Start focusing on loving God. Fall in love with Him again. Seeking a selfish agenda in prayer only proves you have lost your first love. But if your first love is restored, your first "works" is restored along with it (Revelation 2:4-5). And with that, you will begin to seek God's will again, making him the center of your life. Our prayers become more powerful and effective when we align our motives with God's will. Jesus said in John 15:7, "If you remain in me and my words remain in you, ask whatever you wish, and it will be done for you." When our hearts align with God's will, we can trust that our prayers will be answered according to His plans. Aligning our motives with God's will, enables us to cultivate a deeper relationship with Him. It allows us to surrender our desires and plans to His perfect will and to trust Him for the outcomes in our lives.

1. Focus on The Big Picture

Focusing on the big picture is essential for praying with the right motive. Without this focus, your prayers may be limited to your immediate circle. By "immediate circle," I mean yourself, your family, and your loved ones. Looking beyond your personal needs, focusing on God's broader plan for the world and concentrating on the greater good, makes praying with the right motive easier. Additionally, praying for peace, love, and harmony contributes to humanity's well-being.

Living in an environment, a neighborhood, or nation is unwise without covering it in prayer. If anything goes wrong, it will affect you directly or indirectly. Furthermore, peace is not the natural order in any environment. If you see peace anywhere, someone's prayer made it happen. Peace is born and sustained in prayer. Pray for the peace of your own "Jerusalem" and beyond (Psalm 122:6).

2. Seek A Higher Purpose in Prayer

There are higher purposes in prayer that transcend our desires for pleasure and hunger for the mundane. When you seek such higher purposes in prayer, it is a sign that you have matured spiritually, possessing the stature to be used mightily by God for greater purposes. We see this demonstrated in the story of Hannah. I believe Hannah saw a higher purpose than simply her need for a son, she saw a people in need of a Godly priest. Hannah purposed in her heart, should God grant her a son, she would dedicate him to the Lord and God answered her prayer (I Samuel 1:11). In a similar manner, the story is told of a group of American Soldiers preparing for battle during World War II. Facing a fierce fight the next day and aware of the impending danger and the potential loss of lives, they took the night before to pray. Almost all of them prayed in the same way. You might be surprised to learn what they prayed for:

"Lord, tomorrow, we will storm the beaches of Tarawa. Our officers have warned us that this will be a bloody battle. Many of our comrades will be killed. If this must happen, Lord, let those of us who are Christians be the ones to perish. Spare those who do not yet believe; allow them time to choose Christ, in Jesus' name. Amen!" **NEED CITATION FOR THIS QUOTE**

Can you imagine such a prayer? What would motivate someone to pray in that way? These individuals prioritized others and God's purposes over their well-being. They demonstrated a willingness to make sacrifices for others. This is a valuable lesson since few people today are willing to sacrifice for God; in our current era, many people seem less concerned with others and even less so with God's purposes. However, we can hope for a change, starting with improving our approach to prayer.

DON'T STRUGGLE IN PRAYER

Prayer is one of the most challenging spiritual disciplines believers struggle with today. Many people study, relate, and engage in various activities, but few excel in prayer. Numerous churches are known for their effective outreaches, caring welfare systems, or strong teaching ministries, but not many are recognized as praying churches. Even though prayer is essential, it eludes many individuals. The reality is that if you falter in prayer, you will struggle in many other areas of your spiritual life. We must cultivate a heart filled with love, compassion, and selflessness to pray without sin and with the right motive. We must release our egos, fears, and doubts and trust the divine plan. In so doing, we will experience the life changing power of prayer in our lives. How do you avoid struggling in prayer? 1) Allow the Holy Spirit to guide, to nudge, to stir you to pray. You will not always have a perfect moment to pray, but the more you pray, the more you build your prayer muscle, the more you will love to pray and desire to engage in frequent conversations with God. 2) Find a praying church. Become a part of a church that loves to pray or find a prayer partner – look for people who love to pray. 3) We all have 24 hours, schedule a block or small blocks of time throughout your day to pray. Developing a habit of prayer will make it easier to pray.

Reflection

1. What are your motives when you pray? Be honest and write down your motives as they come to mind. Afterward, what do you need to do to ensure you have the right motives when you pray? As you get ready to commune with God, look at what you have written and ask God to highlight and purify your motives. Let love guide your prayers.

Chapter Four
PRAY ACCORDING TO GOD'S PATTERN

To witness significant results with God, you must understand how God operates. A consistent quality of God revealed in the scriptures is His nature as a God of patterns. As a God of patterns, He has well-established methods for executing His will in every aspect. Knowing what He wants you to do and following through is crucial when working with God. However, simply knowing and acting on His wishes isn't sufficient; you must discern His established pattern for accomplishing them. Aligning with God's pattern is essential. To achieve the desired outcomes, God's work must be done in accordance with His ways. This may not be fully understood without grasping God's wisdom. And as you study the Bible, you'll find that God consistently emphasizes these patterns to provide His support. When giving instructions to Moses about the Tabernacle, He ensured that Moses would adhere to the delivered pattern:

> *"And the Lord spake unto Moses, saying, Speak unto the children of Israel, that they bring me an offering: of every man that giveth it willingly with his heart ye shall take my offering. And this is the offering which ye shall take of them; gold, and silver, and brass, And blue, and purple, and scarlet, and fine linen, and goats' hair, And rams' skins dyed red, and badgers' skins, and shittim wood, Oil for the light, spices for anointing oil, and for sweet incense, Onyx stones, and stones to be set in the ephod, and in the breastplate. And let them make me a sanctuary; that I may dwell among them. According to all that I shew thee, after the pattern of the tabernacle, and the pattern of all the instruments thereof, even so, shall ye make it...Of a talent of pure gold shall he make it, with all these vessels. And look that thou make them after their pattern, which was shewed thee in the mount." Exodus 25:1-9, 39-40*

Here, God provides specific instructions to Moses regarding various worship articles and the Tabernacle. As evident, every detail follows a custom design. Each element had specifications directed by God, from the materials and colors to the items' dimensions.

One might think the specifications were arbitrarily determined when viewed at face value. However, they weren't; God is too meticulous and purposeful to use words carelessly. His wisdom and intelligence surpass such actions. But why would He insist on these specific details? The answer is simple. Patterns. Each pattern serves as a code, revealing specific principles or aspects of God's nature. Thus, violating these patterns would compromise a critical part of God's relationship with humanity. Often, a seemingly insignificant detail may unveil a fundamental principle or ordinance of the Christian faith.

THERE IS A DIVINE PATTERN FOR ANSWERED PRAYERS

There exists a well-established scriptural pattern for prayer. To experience consistent breakthroughs in prayer, we must follow this pattern. Jesus Himself first revealed this pattern. When His disciples asked Him to teach them how to pray, Jesus provided what we know today as the Lord's Prayer.

> *"And it came to pass that, as he was praying in a certain place, when he ceased, one of his disciples said unto him, Lord, teach us to pray, as John also taught his disciples. And he said unto them, When ye pray, say, Our Father which art in heaven, Hallowed be thy name. Thy kingdom come. Thy will be done, as*

> *in heaven, so in earth. Give us day by day our daily bread. And forgive us our sins; for we also forgive every one that is indebted to us. And lead us not into temptation, but deliver us from evil." Luke 11:1-4*

In the Lord's Prayer, Jesus didn't provide a prayer to memorize and recite; He offered a pattern of prayer to follow. In fact, before introducing the Lord's Prayer, Jesus emphasized to His disciples that believers should not repeat prayers, thinking they would be heard because of their many words. Jesus referred to this as "vain repetitions." Instead, Jesus presented a divine pattern for how prayer should be offered.

> *"But when ye pray, use not vain repetitions, as the heathen do: for they think that they shall be heard for their much speaking. Be not ye, therefore, like unto them: for your Father knoweth what things ye have need of, before ye ask him." Matthew 6:7-8*

Jesus explained that you wouldn't be heard due to vain repetition. Unfortunately, many people unknowingly use the Lord's Prayer in a repetitive manner, contrary to Christ's instructions. Let us examine the Lord's Prayer to identify the various components that comprise this prayer pattern. Adhering to these five components ensures that you will be heard and receive a breakthrough in your prayer.

1. Show Reverence for God

Our top priority in prayer must be God, not our needs. This is the first principle revealed in the Lord's prayer, "...Our Father which art in heaven, Hallowed be thy name." Matthew 6:9

The phrase "hallowed be thy name" can be understood as a statement of respect and reverence, expressing a desire for others to treat God's name as holy and sacred. It reflects an acknowledgment of God's holiness and a desire for it to be recognized and honored.

This portion of the Lord's Prayer emphasizes God's glory and our relationship with Him. This process involves acknowledging God as our Father and recognizing the holiness of His name. This reminder underlines that we should do so with reverence and awe when approaching a holy and righteous God. Our goal must be to revere and worship the Almighty God.

Although we approach Him from an intimate position as our Father, we must demonstrate deep reverence and devotion by worshipping Him. We must acknowledge who He is and what He has done. The Psalmist declares: "Bless the Lord, O my soul: and all that is within me, bless his holy name. Bless the Lord, O my soul, and forget not all his benefits:" (Psalm 103:1-2) When you read further in the same chapter of Psalm 103, the psalmist itemizes all the beautiful things God had done for him. This type of prayer is also referred to as the prayer of adoration.

Those who focus solely on their needs miss God; however, those who focus on God find all their needs met. God is all you need to fulfill all your needs. Therefore, when you pray to God, try to reverence, adore, and worship Him before making any requests. Understanding, focusing on, and seeking God will transform your prayer life.

2. Prioritize God's Kingdom

The second emphasis in prayer should be on prioritizing the Kingdom of God. This prayer serves as a reminder that our ultimate goal is to see God's kingdom established on earth and that we should submit to His will in all aspects of our lives. Besides God's glory, His kingdom is of utmost importance to Him. God desires the advancement of His kingdom on earth. He wishes for His values to be replicated across the entire world. That is what is meant by the segment, "Thy kingdom come. Thy will be done on earth, as it is in heaven" (Matthew 6:10).

This prayer embodies consecration and surrender. Consecration means to be set apart for God's use. This process involves dedicating all aspects of our life (body, mind, spirit, career, finances, family, etc.) to God's exclusive use. When you say, "Thy kingdom come, thy will be done on earth..." (Matthew 6:10) you surrender your will and embrace God's will. This action mirrors what Jesus did in Gethsemane (Matthew 26:42). It is imperative that we prioritize the kingdom of God.

In the sixth chapter of Matthew's gospel, Jesus encourages us to seek His kingdom first rather than focusing on our obvious natural human needs. We attract those things as additional rewards for prioritizing the kingdom.

> *"But seek ye first the kingdom of God, and his righteousness; and all these things shall be added unto you." Matthew 6:33*

Your prayer life must reflect your deep passion for God's kingdom. By understanding this principle and mastering its application in prayer, you'll never struggle with unanswered prayer again. This principle made a significant difference in the life of Hannah. Many people discuss Hannah's persistence and passion for prayer (how she prayed with a bitter heart). However, they often overlook that she prioritized the kingdom of God in her prayer. She demonstrated her commitment by vowing to dedicate her unborn child to God.

> *"And she was in bitterness of soul and prayed unto the Lord, and wept sore. And she vowed a vow and said, O Lord of hosts if thou wilt indeed look on the affliction of thine handmaid, and remember me, and not forget thine handmaid, but wilt give unto thine handmaid a man child, then I will give him unto the Lord all the days of his life, and there shall no razor come upon his head." 1 Samuel 1:10-11*

During this particular era, a pronounced deficit of priests resulted in a need for more of the divine word. Consequently, making a vow to God carried immense weight and significance. She exhibited profound wisdom and placed God's wishes above her own, which paved the way for a divine encounter. Consequently, her prayer was accorded a position of prominence in God's purview. Subsequently, God showered her with the blessing of multiple children. This narrative underscores the potency of placing God's kingdom at the forefront of one's prayers.

3. Pray for Your Needs

As we follow the pattern in the Lord's Prayer, we arrive at the third principle, which involves requesting our needs. It is a prayer to "Give us this day our daily bread" (Matthew 6:11). Our daily "bread" can represent various needs, such as food, housing, transportation, employment, or other essentials. This is also known as the prayer of petition. It acknowledges our reliance on God for our daily necessities. This prayer serves as a reminder to trust God for daily provision.

Praying for our needs is not only scripturally supported but also important to God; He is glorified when our needs are met. God is our father, and every father is delighted to care for his children. In addition to delighting in this role, it is also His responsibility. Jesus assures us in His teachings that our requests made in prayer will be granted:

> *"Ask, and it shall be given you; seek, and ye shall find; knock, and it shall be opened unto you: For every one that asketh receiveth; and he that seeketh findeth; and to him that knocketh it shall be opened. Or what man is there of you, whom if his son asks bread, will he give him a stone? Or if he asks a fish, will he give him a serpent? If ye then, being evil, know how to give good gifts unto your children, how much more shall your Father which is in heaven give good things to them that ask him?" Matthew 7:9-11*

When you ask Him for a fish, He will not give you a serpent. In other words, every father is dedicated to meeting the needs of his children. Thus, praying for your needs is not a burden for God.

4. Ask for Forgiveness

The fourth element in this prayer model emphasizes our relationship with God and others. When approaching God, we must request forgiveness for our sins. This prayer acknowledges that, though we are the righteousness of God in Christ (2 Corinthians 5:21), we inevitably make mistakes. Thus, seeking God's forgiveness is not only appropriate and necessary, it is the right thing to do. Additionally, we must forgive all those who have wronged us; otherwise, our prayers will remain unanswered. In Mark's gospel, Jesus clarifies that resolving any unforgiveness or offense in our hearts is crucial for our prayers to be answered. "And when ye stand praying, forgive, if ye have ought against any: that your Father also which is in heaven may forgive you your trespasses. But if ye do not forgive, neither will your Father which is in heaven forgive your trespasses" (Mark 11:25-26). If we fail to forgive others, our transgressions will be held against us, rendering our prayers unanswered.

5. Lead Us Not into Temptation

The next point in the Lord's Prayer addresses praying against temptation and the evil one. The Bible states: "…lead us not into temptation, but deliver us from evil" (Matthew 6:13). This prayer asks God to protect us from temptation and evil. It acknowledges that we are engaged in a spiritual battle and require His strength to defeat the enemy. Additionally, this prayer recognizes the pervasiveness of evil in our world and seeks to assert dominion over the works of darkness. The devil sets traps for God's children, using their lusts, to jeopardize their faith in God. Satan is on a strategic mission characterized by stealing, killing, and destroying. He seeks to pressure individuals into compromises that will result in shame and reproach against the name of God. I submit to you then that it would be foolish not to acknowledge and confront his works decisively through prayer. Sadly, many believers have inadvertently ascribed excessive power to the devil by giving him too much attention and prominence in their lives. This is a severe mistake. While the devil should not hold a prominent position in our prayer lives, it is an even greater mistake to completely ignore his evil actions against us. That is the purpose of this prayer. It seeks God's protective hedge around us and refuge from the enemy's harmful darts. With this prayer, we can stand firm against the devil's attacks and temptations. I implore you, do not become a victim of the enemy's tactics. Remain sensitive and watchful for his traps. Remember, only those who persevere will be granted the crown of life.

6. Give God Thanks

The closing doxology of the Lord's Prayer is a potent affirmation of God's supreme reign, omnipotent power, and majestic glory. "...For thine is the kingdom, and the power, and the glory, for ever. Amen" (Matthew 6:13). It underscores the necessity of concluding every prayer with expressions of gratitude, creating a pleasing symmetry in our spiritual communications — akin to a beautifully crafted sandwich. Our prayers should be bookended with praise, ensuring our supplications bring delight to God and fulfill their intended purpose.

The Lord's Prayer stands as a timeless and effective blueprint for prayer. As we have explored, it embodies principles of adoration, dedication, request, intercession, and protection (spiritual warfare). It offers a roadmap for engaging God in prayer and experiencing a purposeful and profound spiritual connection with Him. As we align our prayers with this exemplary model imparted by Jesus, I have faith that our lives will bear witness to remarkable breakthroughs in prayer.

Reflection

1. Have you ever considered that God is a God of patterns? In this chapter, I have outlined the pattern we often refer to as the Lord's Prayer. You may have this prayer memorized. However, as you meditate on Matthew 6:9-13, pray the pattern outlined. Let this pattern become a habitual part of your prayer life.

Chapter Five
PERSISTENCE AND FERVENCY IN THE PLACE OF PRAYER

Persistence is key to prayer. To understand the subject of prayer, you must grasp the concept of persistence. The importance of persistence in prayer becomes evident through Jesus' teachings. Some of Jesus' disciples were former followers of John the Baptist (John 1:40) who already knew something about prayer from following John. John had taught them how to pray, so they asked Jesus to teach them, just as John also taught his disciples. Jesus presented them with the Lord's Prayer—a pattern to follow rather than a prayer to recite. After revealing the Lord's prayer pattern, Jesus quickly delves into persistence. *"And it came to pass that, as he was praying in a certain place, when he ceased, one of his disciples said unto him, Lord, teach us to pray, as John also taught his disciples. And he said unto them, When ye pray, say, Our Father which art in heaven, Hallowed be thy name. Thy kingdom come. Thy will be done, as in heaven, so in earth. Give us day by day our daily bread. And forgive us our sins; for we also forgive every one that is indebted to us. And lead us not into temptation, but deliver us from evil."* Luke 11:1-5

Before asking Jesus to teach them how to pray, they had observed Him praying numerous times. Jesus had just finished praying when they made their request. By observing Jesus pray, they realized there was more to prayer than their current knowledge. From this, we can deduce three things:

1. The disciples observed, admired and were impressed by Jesus's prayer and believed it was as profound an experience as John's, if not more.

2. Instinctively and through observation, the disciples understood that Jesus's prayer life was highly effective, yielding remarkable results. This was evident in the miracles that accompanied His ministry. They recognized that Jesus' prayer life was the secret to the power and influence of His ministry.

3. They desired to learn to pray like Jesus, with an aim to achieve similar results.

PERSISTENCE IS A GAME CHANGER

In response to his followers' request, "teach us to pray," Jesus taught them the value of persistence. To illustrate this, Jesus shared a story about a man who needed provisions to entertain his guests. The man asked a friend for three loaves of bread. However, since it was already late at night and the friend was in bed with his children, he refused to help. Nevertheless, due to his persistence, the friend eventually got up and provided everything he needed:

> *"And he said unto them, Which of you shall have a friend, and shall go unto him at midnight, and say unto him, Friend, lend me three loaves; For a friend of mine in his journey is come to me, and I have nothing to set before him? And he from within shall answer and say, Trouble me not: the door is now shut, and my children are with me in bed; I cannot rise and give thee. I say unto you, Though he will not rise and give him because he is his friend, yet because of his importunity he will rise and give him as many as he needeth." Luke 11:5-8*

The word "importunity" refers to persistence. The Amplified version of Luke 11:8 provides additional insight:

"I tell you, although he will not get up and supply him anything because he is his friend, yet because of his shameless persistence and insistence, he will get up and give him as much as he needs." Luke 11:8 (AMP). These words are powerful; It says, "...because of his shameless persistence and insistence..."

Notice: This man's friend said he didn't want anyone to trouble him, the door was already shut, and he had gone to bed with his children; he wouldn't want to disturb their sleep. If you are a parent with little kids, I am sure you will understand this man. However, the point is that he had so many legitimate excuses not to get out of bed to provide his friend with those three loaves of bread. But because his friend wouldn't give up, he had to come out, despite all the inconveniences.

This is what it means to persist in prayer. Persistence is a game changer. If you master persistence, you've learned a compelling success factor. Jesus further emphasized persistence:

> *"And I say unto you, Ask, and it shall be given you; seek, and ye shall find; knock, and it shall be opened unto you. For every one that asketh receiveth; and he that seeketh findeth; and to him that knocketh it shall be opened. If a son shall ask bread of any of*

you that is a father, will he give him a stone? or if he asks a fish, will he for a fish give him a serpent?"
Luke 11:9-11

I love how Luke 11:9 is rendered in the Amplified version:

"...Ask and keep on asking and it shall be given you; seek and keep on seeking, and you shall find; knock and keep on knocking and the door shall be opened to you."

PERSISTENCE DEFINED

Asking and continuously asking guarantees answered prayers. This defines persistence in prayer. To persist in prayer means maintaining focus despite difficulty or discouragement. Some people like to use the acronym P.U.S.H for this concept. P.U.S.H stands for Pray Until Something Happens!

Persistence in prayer means refusing to take "no" for an answer. You won't always be motivated to pray but must continue praying to receive answers. Persistence in prayer stretches your faith in God to obtain results. Prayer is a rare privilege and a responsibility that should never be taken for granted.

Surprisingly, humans are God's only creatures with the legal right to pray and make things happen on earth.

One of our greatest privileges as believers is prayer, which has the ability to effect changes in our world. This isn't a matter of probability but certainty. If we pray, we will make things happen.

That is why we need an in-depth understanding of the role and power of persistence in prayer. With persistence, you won't need external motivation to pray, you will pray regardless of and in spite of the circumstances happening around you, whether or not you have a problem. Those who wait for external motivation before they pray won't develop a consistent prayer life. It takes persistence to be proactive, to overcome human weaknesses and excuses that attempt to limit your prayer life.

Persistent prayer involves praying despite any factors that could deter you. Wherever persistence is required, some form of resistance is present. God wouldn't expect you to persist unless He knew you would face resistance. Rest assured, persistence can overcome resistance, regardless of the circumstances.

WHY YOU MUST PERSIST

The purpose of persistence in prayer is to sustain the discipline, tenacity, and focus required to commune with God and drive God's agenda in prayer. That means we can develop a robust prayer life despite the limitations or excuses stemming from our weak human nature. Remember, "...the spirit is willing, but the body is weak" (Mark 14:38). Jesus prioritized prayer and heaven's purposes on earth more than anything else.

Most prayers are unanswered because they require more than you can give. It requires sacrificing the pleasures of life in order to obtain the treasure. Hannah was not willing to leave Shiloh, the place she had journeyed to, the place she had gone to offer sacrifices, until she received an answer to her request. She was not interested in food; Hannah came to a place of sacrifice and surrender (I Samuel 1). It is important to have staying power, giving what it takes regarding prayer. We need the Holy Spirit's help in our prayer life. The Holy Spirit will guide us in praying for what we should do and, in the manner necessary to see results.

> *"Likewise, the Spirit also helpeth our infirmities: for we know not what we should pray for as we ought: but the Spirit itself maketh intercession for us with groanings which cannot be uttered." Romans 8:26*

THE WIDOW WHO WOULD NOT LET GO

In Luke 18, Jesus shared a parable about a persistent widow who wouldn't give up. Her actions likely represent the best example of persistence. Jesus began his discussion by emphasizing that people ought to pray and not faint. This woman had lost her husband. It seemed as if she knew her enemy and sought justice. She had no peace and decided to pursue redress in court. Unfortunately, the judicial system did not favor her. The judge, who neither feared God nor regarded man, would not address her concerns. However, because the woman persisted, the unjust judge finally relented. He had no other choice.

> *"And he spake a parable unto them to this end, that men ought always to pray, and not to faint; Saying, There was in a city a judge, which feared not God, neither regarded man: And there was a widow in that city; and she came unto him, saying, Avenge me of mine adversary. And he would not for a while: but afterward, he said within himself, Though I fear not God, nor regard man; Yet because this widow troubleth me, I will avenge her, lest by her continual coming she weary me. And the Lord said, Hear what the unjust judge saith. And shall not God avenge his elect, which cry day and night unto him, though he bear long with them? I tell you that he will avenge them speedily." Luke 18:1-8*

This widow faced significant resistance, but as the judge admitted, he didn't want to get worn out by her continual requests. That is an excellent example of persistence! And that is what prayer demands. To achieve outstanding results through prayer, you must be determined and persistent like the widow woman who refused to accept "no" for an answer.

WHAT DISTINGUISHED ELIJAH

Elijah the prophet differentiated himself from the people of his time. He prayed that there would be no rain and there was none for three and a half years. Elijah did this to redirect the entire nation of Israel back to Jehovah, their God. The book of James lets us know he did it through his persistent and fervent prayer.

"...The effectual fervent prayer of a righteous man availeth much. Elias was a man subject to like passions as we are, and he prayed earnestly that it might not rain: and it rained not on the earth by the space of three years and six months." James 5:16-17

"...The heartfelt *and* persistent prayer of a righteous man (believer) can accomplish much [when put into action and made effective by God—it is dynamic and can have tremendous power]. James 5:16b (AMP)

Persistent prayer involves heartfelt and continuous communication. It is not a fleeting endeavor. When you have a matter to pray about, remain focused until it is resolved. That approach exemplifies Elijah's actions. He prayed until the heavens were closed. And after those three and a half years, he competed with the prophets of Baal on Mount Carmel. He prayed for rain after calling down fire to prove that Jehovah is his God. As mentioned in the book of James, he prayed again, and the heaven gave rain:

> *"And he prayed again, and the heaven gave rain, and the earth brought forth her fruit." James 5:18*

YOU CAN DO IT

Elijah was a man similar to us. He experienced emotions, faced challenges, and dealt with fears; he likely had bills to pay and felt hungry at times. Scripture reveals that he even experienced depression at times (1 Kings 19:4), further demonstrating his similarity to us, yet, through his prayer, he had the power to stop the rain from falling and to bring it forth when necessary. How did he achieve this? The answer lies in his persistent and fervent prayers.

Persistent prayer transforms ordinary individuals into influential people capable of achieving extraordinary results. Elijah's exceptional results stemmed from his persistent prayers. He refused to accept "no" for an answer, and he never gave up or succumbed to his human weaknesses. He grasped the concept of "continue in prayer" (Colossians 4:2). In 1 Thessalonians 5:17, Paul admonished the believers of Thessalonica to "Pray without ceasing." In my own life, specifically, my journey to obtaining a professional career, I learned and experienced first hand that God honors ceaseless prayers.

PRESS DEEPER IN PRAYER

As you learn to pray without ceasing, pressing deeper into the things of God will become easier. At times you may feel as if God is not hearing you but I encourage you to keep pushing. Don't confuse difficulty with impossibility, if you persist a little bit more, you will get a breakthrough. Even when it seems as if your prayers are not working, don't quit, stay with God; the more it seems as if your prayers are not being answered, just know you are passing through the wilderness, yes, weeping may endure for a night but joy comes in the morning (Psalm 30:5). It's important to understand that God is limitless. There is always more to every facet of life God brings you into! Therefore, expressing your hunger through prayer will set you apart from the crowd. The passion and extent of your request determine God's framework of operations in your life (Ephesians 3:20). Like Elijah, you must see beyond the physical, finding the motivation to tarry and pay the price for the deeper things of God. Your pursuit of God determines how far you go. However, some people may want to stop you. Many well-intentioned believers you encounter may try to quench your hunger and passion for

God; don't let them. Lacking vision, they will try everything to deter you from maintaining your focus and passion for God. You must not let distractions deter you from pursuing God! Rise above the crowd and boldly stand for God! Do not let your circumstances limit you. Deepen your prayer life and seek God's power fervently.

Remain tenacious, passionate, and focused during prayer. Persist in prayer until you witness results. To achieve consistent results and receive answers, pray, pray and pray some more. The Bible tells us that men ought ALWAYS to pray and not to faint or give up (Luke 18:1). This means praying continuously until you see your desired change. Persistent prayers hold great power. As we persist in prayer, we can achieve results. You will experience a significant turnaround in Jesus' name through God's grace as you pray fervently!

Reflection

1. In this chapter I have provided several examples of persons who persisted in prayer. What other examples can you find in the Bible? Are there examples in your own life where you persisted in prayer? Times when you gave up too soon? As you meditate on the Scriptures in this chapter, ask God to help you to be persistent.

Chapter Six

PRAYING THE WORD OF GOD IN FAITH!

The infallible word of God serves as the most vital foundation for answered prayers. We lack answers to prayer because our prayers are not based on the word of God. Prayer isn't about forcing God to act on our behalf; it's an attempt to prioritize God's word. Prayer involves asking God to fulfill His will. While praying, you bring God's word back to Him reminding Him of His promises in your area of need. Since God is committed to His promises, you are more likely to receive answers when you bring His word to Him.

> *"Take with you words, and turn to the Lord: say unto him, Take away all iniquity, and receive us graciously: so will we render the calves of our lips."*
> Hosea 14:2

When our prayers reflect God's intentions and promises we can remain assured that He will respond. God's supernatural intervention in your life necessitates a firm grasp on His word that is relevant to your situation. Being a believer does not guarantee answers to your prayers; you must align your prayers with God's word. We can have the utmost confidence in prayer when we align our requests with God's will, knowing He hears and answers us.

"And this is the confidence that we have in him, that, if we ask anything according to his will, he heareth us: And if we know that he hear us, whatsoever we ask, we know that we have the petitions that we desired of him." 1 John 5:14-15

Prayer begins when we know the will of God. Understanding God's will helps us in how we approach Him in prayer. This provides an advantage in receiving answers to your prayer. The word of God represents His will. This legal document outlines what God can do and what we can ask for. The importance of knowing the word of God for yourself cannot be overstated.

PRAYER REQUIRES FAITH

Faith in God's word guarantees answers. God's word gives birth to faith. To receive answers to your prayers, pray with faith using God's word. Prayer serves as a means to express our faith. Those who believe in God's word experience His glory despite all odds. However, those who don't believe only disgrace themselves. When praying for a specific need, begin with faith rather than simply asking for it. To cultivate faith, seek guidance from God's word on the matter. The scripture states that: "So then faith cometh by hearing, and hearing by the word of God" (Romans 10:17). Faith relies on the revelation of God's word regarding a matter. You cannot assert faith without a revelation from God's word. Otherwise, it would merely be an assumption. Regrettably, numerous Christians rely on assumptions and question why their prayers go unanswered. But faith is not an assumption, rather it is an action rooted in God's word.

GROW IN THE WORD

Praying without first receiving a specific word from the Lord is futile. Having a word on the matter provides a strong foundation for prayer. First, you must learn to seek God's word. Seek a verbal promise from God. Without it, your prayers are fruitless, as God fulfills only His promises. Simply because the written word of God addresses a particular aspect of life does not guarantee it will happen. You must seek beyond the written word and receive God's spoken word. Allow God to guide you on the matter.

Begin with the written word, but faith grows in your heart once you receive a specific word from God. With faith in your heart, you can trust that your prayers will be answered. Remember, *"faith is the substance of things hoped for, the evidence of things not seen"* (Hebrews 11:1). If you have faith, you are settled because possessing the substance or the evidence of something is equivalent to having that thing.

Many believers are unfamiliar with this aspect of faith's dynamics. Before you pray for anything, seek a verbal promise from God. Meditate on God's word in your area of need or challenge until you receive a specific message from Him. When you meditate on God's word you begin to see the frame of the thing you desire; meditate until you are able to see what God is doing. As you do this, your faith becomes automatic. I have witnessed in my congregation various seasons, for example, a season of engagements or a season where women are giving birth. I will often say to a man or woman I know is believing God for marriage to look around and observe what is happening around them. As other men or women around them are becoming engaged, they too can believe for their own engagement. They can believe that God will give them a mate too and should begin to prepare themselves – take action.

The story of Noah is one that has always encouraged my faith. Noah received a word from God to build an ark. He built the ark and after that God sent the animals. Noah had never seen rain before but the fact that God told him to build an ark and the animals came was enough evidence that surely it would rain. Noah obeyed the instructions he received from God (Genesis 6-9). When God instructs us with a promise or revelation from His word then our duty is to trust and watch as God performs his promises in our lives.

YOU CAN RELY ON GOD

We can base our prayer on God's revealed words because He always keeps His promises. God's word is His covenant. Without that, we would lack the confidence to stand on His word as a basis for our prayers. If He is the type to make and break promises, praying confidently would be nearly impossible, no matter how many promises He made to us. The good news is that God is a covenant-keeping God. When He makes a promise to you, you can confidently stake your life on it without feeling disappointed. You can trust that He will fulfill it. He is unlike humans who waver with even the slightest change in circumstances. God's covenant cannot fail, as scripture tells us that God cannot lie.

> *"God is not a man, that he should lie; neither the son of man, that he should repent: hath he said, and shall he not do it? or hath he spoken, and shall he not make it good?" Numbers 23:19*

God's inability to lie means that He cannot break His promises. However, more significantly, when God speaks, and you believe in His words, they manifest. His word has the power to manifest exactly what it conveys. The secret is that an unbreakable oath supports God's word:

> *"Wherein God, willing more abundantly to shew unto the heirs of promise the immutability of his counsel, confirmed it by an oath: That by two immutable things, in which it was impossible for God to lie, we might have a strong consolation, who have fled for refuge to lay hold upon the hope set before us:" Hebrew 6:17-18*

Another remarkable aspect of the word is that God has exalted His word above His name. God's word is a more sure word of prophecy (2 Peter 1:19). The Psalmist puts it this way:

> *"I will worship toward thy holy temple, and praise thy name for thy lovingkindness and for thy truth: for thou hast magnified thy word above all thy name."*
> Psalm 138:2

The Bible says that God's word is settled.

> *"For ever, O Lord, thy word is settled in heaven."*
> Psalm 119:89

God's word, which is already settled in heaven, is meant to resolve any situation you may face. When what is settled in God takes root in your heart, you are genuinely settled. I pray that God's infallible word brings peace to your health, marriage, children, business, and career in Jesus' mighty name!

God kept His word when he promised to bless Sarah with a child. Although it took time, He did not let His word falter due to His oath. He visited Sarah just as He said He would.

> *"And the Lord visited Sarah as he had said, and the Lord did unto Sarah as he had spoken. For Sarah conceived, and bare Abraham a son in his old age, at the set time of which God had spoken to him."*
> Genesis 21:1-2

THE PRAYER OF SOLOMON

In studying Solomon's prayer, we are reminded that we can confidently bring God's promises to Him in prayer. Solomon's prayer provides insight into how to enforce the word in prayer. *"And he stood before the altar of the Lord in the presence of all the congregation of Israel, and spread forth his hands...And said, O Lord God of Israel, there is no God like thee in the heaven, nor in the earth; which keepest covenant, and shewest mercy unto thy servants, that walk before thee with all their hearts: Thou which hast kept with thy servant David my father that which thou hast promised him; and spakest with thy mouth, and hast fulfilled it with thine hand, as it is this day. Now therefore, O Lord God of Israel, keep with thy servant David my father that which thou hast promised him; ...There shall not fail thee a man in my sight to sit upon the throne of Israel; yet so that thy children take heed to their way to walk in my law, as thou hast walked before me."* 2 Chronicles 6:12, 14-16

In the above prayer, Solomon reminded God of his covenant with his father, David. He did not pray based on assumptions or emotions. Instead, he held God accountable for His promise. That is how prayer ought to be prayed to achieve results.

KEYS TO PRAYING THE WORD

Here are a few keys that will help you pray the word of God in faith:

1. Learn to Esteem the Word

To pray effectively the word of God by faith, you need to prioritize God's word. Giving God's word first place in our lives is always the beginning to accessing and enjoying all the resources of the kingdom of God. Everything you need is in the Word of God. It is the custodian of all the blessings of God, packaged and made available for God's children. As Paul says, getting a hold of the word of God will deliver your inheritance to you: *"And now, brethren, I commend you to God, and to the word of his grace, which is able to build you up, and to give you an inheritance among all them which are sanctified."* Acts 20:32

Everything originates in the word of God. The word of God is the foundation of the entire universe, and anything that does not find its basis in the word will not prosper.

> *"In the beginning was the word, and the word was with God, and the Word was God. The same was in the beginning with God. All things were made by him, and without him was not anything made that was made."* John 1:1-3

The Book of Genesis also reveals how God spoke everything into being. As soon as the word left God's mouth, living and non-living forms leaped into existence (Genesis 1:1-2-6). In the eleventh chapter of Hebrews, the author also alludes to the fact that everything originated by the word of God:

> *"Through faith, we understand that the worlds were framed by the word of God so that things which are seen were not made of things which do appear."* Hebrews 11:3

Apart from everything originating from the word of God, everything is sustained by the word of God. God's word holds everything in its place, visible and invisible—both living and nonliving. Without the word of God, nothing can hold together. Remember, Jesus Christ is the living word by whom everything fits together:

> *"Who being the brightness of his glory, and the express image of his person, and upholding all things by the word of his power..."* Hebrews 1:3

To always receive answered prayer, you must learn to give the word of God its proper place. Decide to esteem God's word more than anything else, no matter how valuable it is to you.

What does it mean to esteem God's word in your life? It means to revere the word, placing the highest value on it. To esteem God's word is to make it the final authority in your life. In other words, every decision you make is governed and influenced by the word of God. Esteeming God's word in your heart and life will position you for answered prayers.

That was the life of Job: He valued God's word more than everything you can think of. He loved God's word more than his daily necessities, including breakfast, dinner, and lunch. To him, God's word was the real big deal:

> *"Neither have I gone back from the commandment of his lips; I have esteemed the words of his mouth more than my necessary food." Job 23:12*

2. Hold on to a Scriptural Promise

The second way to pray using the word is to tie your prayer request with a promise found in scripture. When you have a prayer request, search for the relevant scriptures where God has made a related promise. Once you find the appropriate scriptures, meditate on them until they become a revelation. Don't pray with vain repetition (as the Bible calls it – Matthew 6:7); instead, pray with the revealed word concerning your specific request. Understand that your revelation determines your faith's direction, which influences the outcomes of your prayers. In the Book of Acts, there is a story about a man who had been lame. He listened to Paul preach the gospel. As Paul proceeded, he noticed that the man had faith in being healed. Paul then helped him up, and the man was completely healed.

> *"And there sat a certain man at Lystra, impotent in his feet, being a cripple from his mother's womb, who never had walked: The same heard Paul speak: who steadfastly beholding him, and perceiving that he had faith to be healed, Said with a loud voice, Stand upright on thy feet. And he leaped and walked."*
> *Acts 14:8-10*

The man had "faith to be healed." It could have been faith to prosper or be protected, but we are told he had faith to be healed. This implies that Paul must have preached on divine healing, activating his faith in healing. Faith comes by hearing (Romans 10:17). The implication for us is that having faith in a specific area requires the revealed word concerning the area. The revealed word is simply the word of God becoming alive to you in which you see and interact with the word. This results in experiential knowledge beyond the written pages. The Greek word for it is rhema. The Bible discusses the word of God becoming flesh and dwelling among men.

> *"And the Word was made flesh, and dwelt among us, (and we beheld his glory, the glory as of the only begotten of the Father,) full of grace and truth." John 1:14*

Having the revealed word in an area indicates that you have been listening to the word of God concerning that topic. Faith is borne in your heart when you have the revealed word in an area. Tying your prayer to the revealed word guarantees answered prayers. Again, don't merely tie your prayer to an ordinary promise; connect it to the revealed word.

3. Use the Word of God as a Weapon

In addition to enforcing the word of God in prayer or connecting your prayer to the revealed word, we must learn how to engage in spiritual warfare using the word of God. Demonic forces can withhold the manifestation of your answers. Many people fail to realize that their prayers can be hindered. Satan can hinder your sincere efforts and the answers to your prayers. Paul shared an experience of how Satan hindered his effort.

> *"Wherefore we would have come unto you, even I Paul, once and again; but Satan hindered us." 1 Thessalonians 2:18*

Instead of debating whether Satan can hinder the manifestation of your prayers, take action and counteract his activities against your prayers. Just as Jesus overcame temptation with the word you can overcome Satan's hindrances by "warring" with the revealed word. Jesus in combatting the enemy responded by using the word, "it is written" (Luke 4:1-13). Expressing God's word in prayer ignites a supernatural force that transforms your efforts into a powerful weapon to defeat your enemies. Use the word of God to defeat the devil!

4. Commit to Doing the Word

Another crucial aspect is putting God's word into practice. Putting God's Word into practice means applying it in your life. You will see results as you apply God's Word in your life. Praying with faith is just the beginning. Faith necessitates action to yield the complete results of our prayers. This concept is known as a corresponding action. When your action aligns with your prayer, they transform your desires into tangible outcomes. Remember, faith without works is dead (James 2:17). Therefore, you will not achieve the desired results without supporting your prayers with faith-driven actions.

I've shared many insights about the importance of the word of God in your prayer, but without addressing this balance, you may still face frustration, and many of your prayers might remain unanswered. The Word of God is effective when we put it into practice. You might pray with faith using the word of God, but without accompanying it with corresponding actions, your efforts could crumble like a house of cards.

Praying with the word can also involve reading or reciting the scripture prayerfully, allowing the verse's meaning to inspire your thoughts and shape your prayer. Praying the word enhances your prayer life by introducing a fresh perspective. It's well-known that prayer is a conversation with God. Thus, it's crucial to use the word of God as the foundation for our dialogue. Aligning our prayers with God's word increases the likelihood of receiving answers. Praying the word of God in faith can and will dramatically affect your prayer life.

As you pray the word, it elevates your relationship with God to a higher level. As you speak and pray God's truth back to Him, prayer becomes easier, more enjoyable, and more rewarding. Your faith grows and rises to a new height in authoritative strength and confidence as you build up your capacity in God's word. When we truly begin to pray according to God's will we will see an increasing number of our prayers answered for God's glory (1 John 5:14-15). This will become your story!

Reflection

1. A differentiator when it comes to prayer is praying the word of God in faith. Take a moment to review the scriptures outlined in this chapter. Write out and meditate on each scripture. What is the Holy Spirit saying to you about these scriptures? Ask the Holy Spirit to help you to exercise the faith you have and then to increase your faith.

2. Consider a situation you are facing. Search the scriptures and find a story or verse that is similar to what you are encountering. Use those scriptures as a point of reference and begin to pray those scriptures over your situation. For example, if you are believing God for healing, then find scriptures on healing, begin to meditate and pray those scriptures over your circumstance.

SCAN ME

Chapter Seven
THE PRAYER OF AGREEMENT AND INTERCESSION

There are various types of prayers revealed to us in the scripture. The Bible emphasizes consistently praying with all kinds of prayer and supplication in the Spirit:

> *"Pray at all times (on every occasion, in every season) in the Spirit, with all [manner of] prayer and entreaty..." (Ephesians 6:18, AMP).*

The word "manner" refers to various types of prayer that can be prayed to achieve results. Each form of prayer is designed to address multiple needs or purposes. Generally, we can divide prayer into two categories. The first category is individual prayer, involving a single person. The second category is corporate prayer, in which multiple people pray together for personal or corporate needs. These prayers may include the prayer of faith, the prayer of thanksgiving, the prayer of intercession, the prayer of agreement, among others.

THE PRAYER OF AGREEMENT

In this chapter I emphasize the importance of the prayer of agreement. The prayer of agreement involves coming together with two or more people and agreeing on a matter for a desired outcome. It entails uniting in prayer and combining your faith with another for a specific need. While praying alone has value, sometimes you need another person's faith to join with yours to overcome obstacles. In other words, addressing some issues requires a collaborative and focused effort.

It is important to first understand the concept of agreement to comprehend the prayer of agreement. The term 'agree' signifies harmony, alignment and synergy. As the Bible asserts, for collaboration to be successful, there must be agreement: "Can two walk together, except they be agreed?" (Amos 3:3)

The act of two or more people coming together to agree on a specific situation is incredibly powerful. Throughout the scriptures we see how the power and role of agreement created supernatural breakthroughs in a range of life situations.

ROOTED IN THE WORD

In the gospels, we find several instances of people agreeing together in prayer. Jesus Himself taught the concept of the prayer of agreement. He stated: *"Again I say unto you, That if two of you shall agree on earth as touching anything that they shall ask, it shall be done for them of my Father which is in heaven. For where two or three are gathered together in my name, there am I in the midst of them."* Matthew 18:19

Heaven will support our agreement with answers if we agree on earth about anything. Isn't that incredible? That is a powerful promise from God's word. When Jesus speaks, He means every word. He is not like a man who says one thing but means another. Jesus speaks with sincerity, truth and clarity. Thus, when He says "something will be done," it will be done.

Jesus encouraged his disciples to practice the prayer of agreement, and assured them their prayers would be answered. Jesus even sought agreement in prayer with His disciples. Facing the danger of death, He asked three of His closest followers to come and pray with Him.

> *"And he took with him Peter and the two sons of Zebedee, and began to be sorrowful and very heavy. Then saith he unto them, My soul is exceeding sorrowful, even unto death: tarry ye here, and watch with me."* Matthew 26:37-38 Though they were sleepy and unable to pray with Him, Jesus desired their agreement in prayer.

THE POWER OF AGREEMENT IN PRAYER

There is power in praying together. When two or more people pray in agreement, the strength of their prayers is amplified, and the power of their faith is multiplied. In essence, praying together before God has a multiplicative effect. When two people join forces, they accomplish more than one individual can alone.

> *"How should one chase a thousand, and two put ten thousand to flight, except their Rock had sold them, and the Lord had shut them up?"* Deuteronomy 32:30

In many prayer meetings and circumstances, I have witnessed the collective power of group prayer.

This level of power is not accessible to an individual praying alone. Regardless of a person's anointing, they cannot access this same level of power as a group of believers. Individuals operate within their anointing, while groups operate within a collective anointing. Thus, there lies the advantage. We see this in the collective prayers of the early church that resulted in the shared power they possessed.

In Acts 1:14, the early church agreed: "These all continued with one accord in prayer and supplication, with the women, and Mary the mother of Jesus, and with his brethren." This unity formed the foundation of the early church, and through their united prayers, they experienced the outpouring of the Holy Spirit on the day of Pentecost (Acts 2:1-4). In the fourth chapter of the Book of Acts, after being arrested, maltreated, and threatened for healing a lame man at the Beautiful Gate (Acts 3), they returned and prayed in agreement with their fellow believers.

> *"And being let go, they went to their own company and reported all that the chief priests and elders had said unto them. And when they heard that, they lifted up their voice to God with one accord, and said, Lord, thou art God, which hast made heaven and earth, and the sea, and all that in them is...And now, Lord, behold their threatenings: and grant unto thy servants, that with all boldness they may speak thy*

> *word, By stretching forth thine hand to heal; and that signs and wonders may be done by the name of thy holy child Jesus. And when they had prayed, the place was shaken where they were assembled together; and they were all filled with the Holy Ghost, and they spake the word of God with boldness." Acts 4:23-24, 29-32*

The early church understood the power of agreement in prayer and witnessed many remarkable results. When we follow their example, we too can experience breakthroughs in prayer.

PRAYING TOGETHER CAN CHANGE EVERYTHING

It's truly breathtaking to behold the miraculous outcomes and untapped potential that our faith can achieve when we join forces in prayer. A fellow believer confided in me not long ago about his struggle with an intimidating life challenge. The problem appeared insurmountable, and the sheer magnitude of the situation nearly overwhelmed him, leaving him on the brink of despair. The circumstance made him realize the urgency for divine assistance. Having learned about the profound power of joining forces in prayer, he chose to apply it. He reached out to a trusted friend, and together, they committed to a joint prayer session.

The result of their shared prayer was nothing short of astonishing. In the subsequent days, a significant shift occurred. Doors that had previously been shut began to swing open, obstacles vanished, and divine favor was miraculously activated. It was as though the heavens had shifted in response to their collective prayers. Not only did they witness breakthroughs in their situations, but they also saw the transformative effect of united prayer in the lives of others. As they expanded their prayers beyond their individual needs, interceding on behalf of their families, friends, and communities, a simultaneous wave of healing, restoration, and transformation swept through the lives of those they prayed for. The speed at which God worked through their combined prayers to fulfill their needs and that of others was awe-inspiring.

Through this experience, we've gained a profound understanding of the true power of united prayer. When two or more believers unite in prayer, their prayers have greater influence and authority. Their collective faith and unity catalyze miracles as though by divine alchemy. In essence, when we pray in agreement with one another, the potency of our prayers is magnified, and our appeals reach God's throne with amplified intensity.

This experience underscores that united prayer is more than just a religious ritual—it's a formidable spiritual tool. It is a comforting reminder that we're not alone in our struggles and challenges; we have fellow believers ready to stand alongside us in life's battles. Together, we can surmount any hurdle and experience the supernatural intervention of our heavenly Father.

AGREEMENT IN PRAYER REQUIRES UNITY

To pray effectively, unity is essential. While there are other important elements, unity remains crucial. Without unity, agreement in prayer cannot be achieved. Unity brings about divine alignment. Unity introduces a powerful force to any situation. Notice that the Bible says that where two or three are gathered together in His name, He is in their midst

(Matthew 18:20). In other words, God is present when we, as believers, gather and unite in one heart with the Lord or in His name through prayer. Whenever He is present, everything becomes settled. When He is present among us, no situation can withstand Him, ensuring the effectiveness of our prayers. That is the most beautiful aspect of unity. Prioritize unity if you want God to be present in your family and home.

Striving for unity is a fundamental step toward answered prayers. No force can withstand or hinder the power of unity in prayers. When a group is united, nothing is impossible for them. That is why the devil aims to create discord between you and your spouse. By disrupting your unity, he undermines the balance in your home, creating an opportunity for defeat. His goal is to cause your family to fall apart completely. He constantly whispers in your ear, encouraging you to say the wrong things and make poor decisions. And if you are not careful, you may start to believe and act according to these malicious thoughts. Consequently, you must cast aside those thoughts and remain committed to your spouse. This entails facing any challenges in your home together and overcoming them.

Jesus also prayed for unity among His disciples and, by extension, the entire body of Christ. He knew that the force of disunity would neutralize the power available through His death, burial, resurrection, and ascension. Therefore, He prayed:

> *"...that they may be one, even as we are one: I in them, and thou in me, that they may be made perfect in one;" John 17:22-23*

In every instance in scripture involving the prayer of agreement, participants were in "one accord." Once that condition was met, a tremendous release of power occurred on their behalf. A prime example is the day of Pentecost. As they prayed in unity, the Holy Spirit descended upon them:

> *"And when the day of Pentecost was fully come, they were all with one accord in one place. And suddenly, there came a sound from heaven as of a rushing mighty wind, and it filled all the house where they were sitting. And there appeared unto them cloven tongues like as of fire, and it sat upon each of them. And they were all filled with the Holy Ghost, and began to speak with other tongues, as the Spirit gave them utterance." Acts 2:1-4*

One of the things I have observed is that unity activates God's blessings. In the book of Psalms, David discussed the blessings of God that can only be realized through unity.

> *"Behold, how good and how pleasant it is for brethren to dwell together in unity! It is like the precious ointment upon the head, that ran down upon the beard, even Aaron's beard: that went down to the skirts of his garments; As the dew of Hermon, and as the dew that descended upon the mountains of Zion: for there the Lord commanded the blessing, even life for evermore." Psalm 133:1-3*

God does not bestow blessings in the presence of discord. This is one reason why many people do not receive God's blessings. Unity is a powerful force, not only in prayer but also in life. In your life, embrace the power of unity. In the book of Genesis, we see a certain group of people from that era who decided to build a tower reaching the heavens (Genesis 11:1-6). Though their goal opposed God's intentions, their unity and shared language made them unstoppable.

> *"And the LORD said, Behold, the people is one, and they have all one language; and this they begin to do: and now nothing will be restrained from them, which they have imagined to do." Genesis 11:6*

FAITH MUST BE IN PLACE

For the prayer of agreement to be effective, faith is essential. As mentioned in the Bible, without faith, it is impossible to please God (Hebrews 11:6). Faith forms the foundation of our prayers of agreement and enables us to trust that God will answer our unified prayers. Faith facilitates agreement between any two individuals. Only when two people share a belief can they genuinely agree. If one person lacks belief, their prayer will be ineffective. Even if you physically join hands in prayer, without shared faith, there is no unity and, therefore, no results. When we pray, we must have faith in His Word and promises. Once you've reached an agreement, anticipate positive outcomes from your prayers, despite any potential delays in their manifestation. At times, it may seem as though the agreed-upon outcome is not materializing; however, remain steadfast and unwavering, understanding that God will never break His promise.

AGREEMENT AND INTERCESSION

We can come into agreement and pray with and for others and not just for ourselves. While we may sometimes agree on matters that directly affect us, praying with others for their needs is a valuable experience all believers should embrace. We can engage in the ministry of intercession to pray for others.

Intercessory prayer involves presenting the needs of others to God. In intercession, God invites us to pray for those close and far from us. Sometimes, you may know their needs when interceding; at other times, you may not know. Regardless, your focus remains on bringing the needs of others before God. Surprisingly, you might be the only one praying for these individuals. Intercession offers a unique opportunity to join those who advance Kingdom causes.

One of the functions of an intercessor is to bridge the gap between two parties, God and humanity. The Bible frequently refers to intercessors as watchmen. They can watch over families, organizations, cities, and entire nations in this capacity. Intercessors advocate for matters of heavenly interest until victory is achieved.

> *"I have set watchmen upon thy walls, O Jerusalem, which shall never hold their peace day nor night: ye that make mention of the Lord, keep not silence, And give him no rest, till he establish, and till he make Jerusalem a praise in the earth."* Isaiah 62:6-7

The prayer of intercession is among the most powerful ways to impact the lives of others positively. Even Jesus practiced intercession during His time on earth. Jesus' prayer of intercession sustained Peter after he denied Christ.

> *"And the Lord said, Simon, Simon, behold, Satan hath desired to have you, that he may sift you as wheat: But I have prayed for thee, that thy faith fail not: and when thou art converted, strengthen thy brethren."* Luke 22:31-32

Intercession also facilitated Peter's escape from the prison cell.

> *"Peter therefore was kept in prison: but prayer was made without ceasing of the church unto God for him."* Acts 12:5

The prayer of intercession holds significance for our communities, nations, and political leaders. In 1 Timothy 2:1-2, we're encouraged to intercede "for all people," "for kings" and "for all that are in authority." Through intercessory prayer, we can partner with God to positively impact the lives of others. When you engage in intercession with a clear sense of urgency regarding what is truly required, you are maintaining the consistent prayer necessary to advance God's purposes on earth. Your contribution, whether through intercession or agreement with others in prayer, is significant to the promotion and well-being of others.

IT MADE THE DIFFERENCE

This story revolves around two friends, Jenny and Franca. Franca found herself battling to pay her bills, an utterly overwhelming ordeal. On the other hand, Jenny had employment but didn't provide enough income to handle her mounting debts. One fateful day, these two friends turned to prayer, beseeching God to furnish the necessary financial means to settle their bills and ease Jenny's fiscal strain.

Surprisingly, following their heartfelt prayer, Jenny, who had been grappling with financial stress, received an unexpected bonus at her workplace. The bonus precisely matched the total amount required to clear her outstanding bills. Franca, too, received a monetary blessing that gave her the ability to pay her bills, as well as, assist her family members in need.

In my experience, there is no denying the significant role of agreement in prayers. Like Jenny and Franca, these prayers can certainly make a difference in your life. God is impartial and does not differentiate among His children. The Bible asserts that when we pray in unity, we possess the power to move mountains (Matthew 17:20). There is no boundary to what we can achieve when we choose to pray collectively. Praying in harmony with others can magnify our prayers, bolster our faith, and usher in breakthroughs in our lives.

Reflection

1. What unanswered prayer in your life are you tackling? Have you ever considered partnering with a friend, a trusted confidante, an intercessor, a family member, a pastor, someone? Why not try the prayer of agreement, unite with a prayer partner and together bring your request before God.

SCAN ME

Chapter Eight
AN UNUSUAL LIFE OF SERVICE TO THE LORD

Faithful and sacrificial service to God dramatically influences the results of our prayers. God's plan for our lives is that we serve Him wholeheartedly. His desire for us is that we utilize our distinct gifts and talents to serve Him and humanity. When God sees that we are willing to serve Him, to accept His gift of salvation, He unlocks His treasures and bestows abundant blessings upon us. In studying the Israelites' exodus from Egypt, a parallel to our salvation experience, we see how God instructed Moses to request from Pharaoh the release of His people to serve Him.

> *"And thou shalt say unto him, The Lord God of the Hebrews hath sent me unto thee, saying, Let my people go, that they may serve me in the wilderness: and, behold, hitherto thou wouldest not hear."* Exodus 7:16

When we accept Jesus Christ as our Lord and Savior, we become believers and are now accepted as God's beloved. We become members of His body, of His flesh, and of His bones (Ephesians 5:30). We are united with God in Christ. His love for us is unconditional and there is nothing we can do to make God love us more or less. However, those who serve God catch His attention and have access to untold benefits. For example, God is dedicated to safeguarding His kingdom on earth and those most valuable to Him. He will go to great lengths to protect those who serve Him.

> *"No weapon that is formed against thee shall prosper; and every tongue that shall rise against thee in judgment thou shalt condemn. This is the heritage of the servants of the Lord, and their righteousness is of me, saith the Lord."* Isaiah 54:17

The scripture clearly states that this level of protection is the heritage of God's servants. If we serve God, we can anticipate that any plans the enemy devises against us will not succeed. God will prioritize and defend those who serve Him.

In life we often prioritize things and people according to their value to us. In a country like the United States of America, the state provides additional security detail for its serving officials. A person's level of usefulness to the state or nation dictates the level of security. The President of the United States of America is one of the most protected persons on the planet. Unlike an ordinary citizen, the nation goes to great lengths to ensure the President's protection. Of course, there are safety protocols in place to keep everyone safe. However, officials actively serving the state become a top priority.

As we serve God, it endears us to Him and grants us certain privileges. Here is a prime example:

> *"And ye shall serve the Lord your God, and he shall bless thy bread, and thy water, and I will take sickness away from the midst of thee. There shall nothing cast their young, nor be barren, in thy land: the number of thy days I will fulfill. I will send my fear before thee and will destroy all the people to whom thou shalt come, and I will make all thine enemies turn their backs unto thee." Exodus 23:25-27*

This portion of scripture implies that a prerequisite to enjoying the promises of God is based on our service to him. Additionally, when we serve others, when we show love, we act on God's behalf and extend his reach to the world. We bring hope to the hurting. Serving the Lord in this manner increases the likelihood of our prayers being answered. Why? Because we are actively pursuing God's will rather than our own.

THE PRAYER OF HEZEKIAH

The Bible offers several examples of the connection between serving God and the kingdom of God and answered prayers. One such story is that of Hezekiah. After serving God for several years, king Hezekiah became gravely ill. God sent a prophet to inform him of his impending death. The prophet told him to put his house in order before his death. However, as soon as the prophet left, Hezekiah turned toward the wall and began to pray, asking God to spare his life based on his faithful service. Surprisingly, God answered Hezekiah's prayer and added fifteen more years to his life. God sent the prophet back to Hezekiah to reverse the edict.

"In those days was Hezekiah sick unto death. And Isaiah the prophet, the son of Amoz came unto him and said unto him; thus saith the Lord, set thine

house in order: for thou shalt die, and not live. Then Hezekiah turned his face toward the wall and prayed unto the Lord, And said, Remember now, O Lord, I beseech thee, how I have walked before thee in truth and with a perfect heart, and have done that which is good in thy sight. And Hezekiah wept sore. Then came the word of the Lord to Isaiah, saying, Go, and say to Hezekiah, Thus saith the Lord, the God of David, thy father, I have heard thy prayer, I have seen thy tears: behold, I will add unto thy days fifteen years. And I will deliver thee and this city out of the hand of the king of Assyria: and I will defend this city. And this shall be a sign unto thee from the Lord, that the Lord will do this thing that he hath spoken."
Isaiah 38:1-7

God remembered Hezekiah. If you want your prayers to draw God's attention then you must serve the Lord.

A LIFE OF SERVICE

To serve in God's kingdom is a lifestyle in which we emulate the practices of Jesus by demonstrating his love to the world and by using our gifts, talents, and resources to address the needs of others. This type of service aligns us to Jesus' mission: "For even the Son of man came not to be ministered unto, but to minister, and to give his life a ransom for many"

(Mark 10:45). Jesus' goal was to serve others, not to be served, in contrast to many of our attitudes today, where we prefer to be served rather than to humble ourselves and serve others.

SERVE PEOPLE

As Christians, we are called to a life of love, complete submission to God, and kindness toward humanity. This is what the cross symbolizes. The cross consists of two sides: the vertical and the horizontal. The vertical side represents our relationship with God, while the horizontal side signifies our relationship with people. As both the vertical and the horizontal sides are held together, similarly, we cannot separate our relationship with God from our relationship with people. In other words, serving others is also a way of serving God. It is a way to touch the heart of God. Claiming to serve God without impacting people's lives, either directly or indirectly, is self-deception.

SERVE FAITHFULLY

The call to serve, to impact people's lives, demands faithfulness. Faithfulness is one of the primary requirements for service. Our service isn't solely measured by the duration of service or our position but by our consistency to our assignment. If we are faithful in our service to God, faithful in advancing

God's purpose on earth, we put ourselves in a posture to experience significant rewards and results to our prayers.

This lesson is illustrated through the parable of the talent (Matthew 25:14-30). The parable of the talent tells the story of a man who planned to go on a journey to a distant land. But before he leaves, he gives three of his servants talents. He gave five talents to one servant, two talents to another, and one talent to the last servant. After a significant period, he returned to assess how they had used the talents entrusted to them. The first and the second servant had diligently worked to double their talents. The master, in commending them said, "Well done, good and faithful servant" (Matthew 25:23).

As for the last servant, who had received one talent and buried it, when the master appeared he merely dug up the single talent he had buried in the ground and presented it to his master. This act was not only unfortunate but cruel and wicked. The master, enraged, punished him for his wickedness and slothful behavior. This servant missed out on an opportunity to multiply his talent. The two servants who had faithfully traded their talents for profits were generously rewarded. In other words, our faithfulness to the talents God has given us is essential for productively serving God.

Faithfulness can be described as dependability, reliability, or loyalty. It is a characteristic or result of the recreated human spirit. As a child of God, you carry the seed of faithfulness in your spirit. Many people are familiar with faith, but we lack knowledge about faithfulness. *While faith involves trusting God, faithfulness means that God trusts you.* The question remains: Can God trust you? Are you dependable enough to fulfill God's purposes on earth? If your answer is yes, then congratulations! If not, you must commit to developing the trait of faithfulness.

SERVE SACRIFICIALLY

Another essential aspect of our service to the Lord is sacrifice. Our calling is not only to serve but to serve sacrificially. In Romans 12:1, we are called to offer ourselves as living sacrifices to God. That entails setting aside our desires and priorities and dedicating ourselves to serving God and others. Serving is one thing, but serving sacrificially is an entirely different thing. Many people do not fully benefit from their service to God due to their failure to understand this crucial distinction. Sacrifice is in the cost. Sacrificial service requires giving up something very precious to you. It involves relinquishing valuable things for the sake of God's kingdom.

In the scriptures, sacrifice is often symbolized by blood. In the Old Covenant, people were commanded to sacrifice animal blood to connect with God. We see this in the way the Tabernacle was designed. Upon entering the door, you first encounter the altar of sacrifice. Without the blood, you cannot gain access. You cannot go further into the Tabernacle. The significance of this sacrifice, required at the door of the Tabernacle, lies in the fact that the path to God's deeper truths involves sacrifice. Our dedication to God should involve a life of sacrifice. At the core of this life of sacrifice is love. A love for God and others should be our primary motivation to serve sacrificially.

Although a life of service and sacrifice can be challenging, it is rewarding and fulfilling. Among the most significant rewards of a life of service and sacrifice is its potential impact on others. Serving with love and compassion empowers us to transform lives and communities, bringing hope and healing to a world needing God's love and grace. Through our service, we can provide hope to those struggling and inspire others to emulate our example of selfless service. Besides its impact on others, a life of service and sacrifice also draws us nearer to God. We serve God and fulfill our purpose as his children by serving others.

WAYS TO SERVE

There are a variety of ways in which we can serve God. Here are a few examples:

1. Serve God through Prayer and Fasting

Prayer is one of the most powerful ways to serve God. I am not referring to asking Him for things. I mean the prayer of devotion. Spending time in fellowship with the Lord ministers to Him (Acts 13:2). Additionally, when we embrace the responsibility of advancing God's kingdom through prayer, we serve Him. A prime example is a woman named Anna. Anna, a widow, and a prophetess, dedicated her entire life to serving God through prayer and fasting.

> *"And there was one Anna, a prophetess, the daughter of Phanuel, of the tribe of Aser: she was of a great age, and had lived with a husband seven years from her virginity; And she was a widow of about fourscore and four years, which departed not from the temple, but served God with fasting and prayers night and day." Luke 2:36-37*

Anna persisted in praying for Christ's appearance until He finally arrived. Another example of someone who served God through prayer is David. David was the king of Israel, yet he prayed several times daily as part of his commitment to God's kingdom.

"Seven times a day do I praise thee because of thy righteous judgments." Psalm 119:164

"Evening, and morning, and at noon, will I pray, and cry aloud: and he shall hear my voice." Psalm 55:17

2. Serve God by Preaching the Gospel

God is eager to share His message of unconditional love with the entire world. He desires that everyone worldwide receives the salvation found in Christ Jesus. We can serve this purpose by sharing the gospel with those for whom Christ died. "For God is my witness, whom I serve with my spirit in the gospel of his Son..." Romans 1:9. I can think of no better way to serve God than to share the gospel with others.

3. Serve God Through Your Giving

One of the most important ways to serve God is through your giving. Through your giving, the gospel can be preached in many places. Advancing the kingdom of God requires financial resources (Zechariah 1:17). Serving God without utilizing your resources is akin to leaving Egypt without silver and gold. Remember, Pharaoh did not want the Israelites to leave Egypt with their resources. However, Moses insisted they needed those resources to serve God

(Exodus 10:26). Don't serve God empty-handed; serve Him with your resources. Dedicate your resources for His glory.

FIND YOUR PATH

There are numerous ways to serve God. Find your unique path by tuning your ear to the Holy Spirit and aligning your life's vision and purpose to include a life devoted to service. A life committed to the service of the Lord holds one of the most potent keys to receiving answers to our prayers. We cannot expect to reap the benefits of our relationship with God without actively serving Him. However, our acts of service mixed with our faithfulness and sacrifice will lead to significant changes in our lives. A life of dedication and selflessness unlocks God's promises and gives us breakthroughs in prayer. Let me assure you, as you incorporate the principles of kingdom service outlined in this book, the grace of God will envelop you in Jesus' name. Always bear in mind that there is a God ready to answer every prayerful soul.

Reflection

1. Have you ever considered how important your acts of service are to receiving answers to your prayers as detailed in this chapter? Are you living a sacrificial lifestyle? Are you diligently serving in the Kingdom? If not, what acts of service might you consider?

2. What are your gifts and talents? Do you remember the parable of the talents? How are you developing the gifts and talents God has given to you?

CONCLUSION

As you can see, I am passionate about Christ's followers receiving answers to their prayers. I hope the mechanisms and principles outlined will encourage you to seek God one more time for your breakthrough. I have applied these principles in my own life and have my own set of testimonies. I want you to have your own testimonies too. Before I leave you to put into practice what you have read I want to note an aspect of God's character, and that is His sovereignty. God is sovereign. I mention God's sovereignty as a way to encourage your hearts on your journey to seeking His promises.

I have learned in my walk with God that His plans are much better than mine. There are times when He calls me to submit my desires to His. In these moments what God is suggesting is not always palatable but in time I come to realize that it is for my good. Indeed, God has a better plan than our plan, and our ability to submit to his will, will make us better and not bitter.

Job, in a moment of despair, stated, "the Lord gave, and the Lord hath taken away; blessed be the name of the Lord" (Job 1:21). It takes discipline to say, "blessed be the name of the Lord." However, when we learn to give thanks for God's ways, it puts us in a posture to proclaim that our trust is wholeheartedly in God and not in what we are asking for. Like the three Hebrew boys who encountered a dire situation and yet with no compromise they stated, "If it be so, our God whom we serve is able to deliver us from the burning fiery furnace, and he will deliver us out of thine hand, O king. But if not, be it known unto thee, O king, that we will not serve thy gods, nor worship the golden image which thou hast set up" (Daniel 3: 17-18).

These Old Testament figures had an unwavering trust in the Almighty God. I submit to you that they trusted God with their last drop of blood, they ultimately trusted that God does all things well. They knew something that we at times struggle with, and that is, God is trustworthy. God can be trusted with our sorrows, our pain, with the details of our lives. As an expression of our faith, we pray. If we pray as we ought, then our prayer helps us align to God's will. What does prayer do? It subjects us, subjects our flesh, and connects us to the spiritual realm. Through prayer God communicates His will to us and helps us stay focused on Him.

God is more concerned about our character development than He is about the outcome of our prayer. Like King David, are we quick to repent (eg., Psalm 51). Like Zacharias and Elisabeth, can we submit to the will of God long enough to have him turn seeming delays into honor? (Luke 1) How about Joseph? Can we endure a pit, betrayal, prison, long enough to be able to say that what was meant for evil God turned it around for good? (Genesis 15) The trials we face as humans are varied and yet this is what I know – God wants to show himself strong on our behalf.

My life is certainly a work in progress. In the midst of my own personal challenges God has processed and is still processing me. God knows the end from the beginning. He is working with the end of our lives in mind, desiring at the end to be able to present us to himself without spot or wrinkle (Ephesians 5:27). As Jesus submitted to the cross, so too must we submit to the will of our heavenly Father. Stay the course and watch as your unanswered prayers are converted to breakthroughs. Keep an open mind, God may choose to answer you not in the way you anticipate, but I am convinced He will answer, and breakthrough is yours, in Jesus' name.

SCAN ME

www.ingramcontent.com/pod-product-compliance
Lightning Source LLC
LaVergne TN
LVHW051842080426
835512LV00018B/3028